Ancestors' Footsteps

The Somme 1916

Ancestors' Footsteps

The Somme 1916

Andrew Rawson

Pen & Sword
MILITARY

First published in Great Britain in 2016 by
PEN AND SWORD MILITARY
an imprint of
Pen and Sword Books Ltd
47 Church Street
Barnsley
South Yorkshire S70 2AS

ISBN 978 1 47386 420 7

A CIP record for this book is available from the British Library.

Printed and bound in England by
CPI Group (UK) Ltd, Croydon, CR0 4YY

Typeset in Times by CHIC GRAPHICS

Pen & Sword Books Ltd incorporates the imprints of
Pen & Sword Books Ltd incorporates the imprints of Pen & Sword
Archaeology, Atlas, Aviation, Battleground, Discovery,
Family History, History, Maritime, Military, Naval, Politics,
Railways, Select, Social History, Transport, True Crime,
Claymore Press, Frontline Books, Leo Cooper, Praetorian Press,
Remember When, Seaforth Publishing and Wharncliffe.

For a complete list of Pen and Sword titles please contact
Pen and Sword Books Limited
47 Church Street, Barnsley, South Yorkshire, S70 2AS, England
E-mail: enquiries@pen-and-sword.co.uk
Website: www.pen-and-sword.co.uk

Introduction

The idea for this book started during a conversation with my friends David and Julie Thomson, who run the No 56 Bed and Breakfast in La Boisselle on the Somme. They encounter many visitors who, while they all have different motives for visiting, fall into two main groups. The first group are genealogists who are exploring their family trees. During their research they have discovered a family member who fought (and often died) in the area and wish to visit their grave or memorial. They also want to see some of the famous sights on the Somme. The second group make frequent visits looking, for a variety of reasons, to expand their knowledge of the battles in 1916.

The topic of conversation moved around to 'what questions do your guests have during their visit to the Somme.' At the end of the discussion it was clear there were three main questions.

The first question is, 'Where are the most interesting sites on the Somme?' The answer would include such places as Newfoundland Memorial Park near Beaumont Hamel, the Lochnagar Crater at La Boisselle, and the Thiepval Memorial to the Missing. It is possible to learn about them in tour books, on the internet or in the museums. They are also well signposted.

The second question is, 'Where is my relative remembered on the Somme?' Again it is relatively easy to discover where a soldier was buried or on which memorial to the missing their name is carved. The Commonwealth War Graves Commission website at www.cwgc.org is easy to navigate and the information is only a few clicks away if you know your relative's name, rank and unit. All the cemeteries and memorials are also well signposted on the ground.

But it was the third question which intrigued me. It was, 'Where did my relative fight on the Somme?' Along with that question would be asked, 'and what were they doing?' The answer to this question can be difficult to find out, especially for the family historian with only a passing interest in the First World War. Although it is relatively easy to discover which unit a soldier served in, finding when and where they fought can be difficult. But finding out the information provides a missing piece of the puzzle about their relative's life.

The options are to study the war diaries kept at the National Archives (previously Public Records Office) in Kew, London or to employ someone to check the records on your behalf. Alternatively, hunt down a division's or regiment's history, if one was printed, and check the details. These options are possible but they can be time-consuming and expensive, particularly for a non-military person coming to terms with army terminology.

After doing the book work, comes the next stage in the discovery process for many people. You see, casualties were rarely buried by their comrades near where they fought. Nearly 90,000 British and Empire soldiers killed on the Somme in 1916 have no known grave and their names are carved on the relevant national memorial. British and South African names are on Thiepval memorial; Australian names are on the Villers-Bretonneux memorial; Canadian names are on the Vimy Ridge memorial, New Zealand names are on the memorial in Caterpillar Valley Cemetery. In some cases the name is carved many miles from where a man fought and died. Some of the men with names on memorials are buried in unknown graves in cemeteries but many others are buried in an unmarked field, where they fought and died.

Casualties who were evacuated from the battlefield often died a few hours or days after they were injured. They were buried by the Royal Army Medical Corps next to the first aid posts, dressing stations and casualty clearing stations, many miles from the front line. Others died at the base hospitals and are buried in one of the huge cemeteries along the French coast. Some even died after reaching a hospital in Britain and are buried in a local churchyard.

This book will help you locate the final piece of the puzzle in the search for your ancestors: 'Where did they fight?' It will take you straight to a viewpoint where you can read the narrative and see where they fought and fell, completing their story in the 1916 battle.

So it is a big thank you to David and Julie on two counts. Firstly, for helping me with the idea for the book and, secondly, for their great hospitality at No 56 Bed and Breakfast in La Boisselle, the Somme.

General Information

The Somme campaign started on 1 July 1916 and ended on 18 November. Fourth Army started the battle but the front was soon divided between the Reserve Army in the north and Fourth Army in the south (the Reserve Army was renamed the Fifth Army at the end of October). Each Army split its front between three corps and each of these covered two to three miles of front. Each corps controlled two or three divisions during an attack.

There were ninety-two corps actions during the offensive and the book has a section covering each one. In a few cases a corps is divided into two, or two corps are merged together. In each section there are five pieces of information:

1. Suggested viewpoints
2. The narrative of the fighting
3. An annotated trench map
4. The divisions' orders of battle
5. Memorials and other points of interest

The viewpoints have been chosen to give a good view of as much of the described action as possible. They are all on (or in a short distance of) a tarmac road because even the shortest downpour covers the dirt tracks with slippery mud. Where possible, readily identifiable features have been chosen to make it easier to locate them. Some viewpoints are cemeteries (both military and civilian) and some are memorials or village crucifixes. Other viewpoints are suitable stopping places by the roadside. Hard-standings are large concrete or stone areas farmers use to store their produce during the harvest season. Pull-ins are smaller areas where it is possible to park a car safely, but not a larger vehicle.

The narrative explains what happened in the area and is used in conjunction with the map. It explains which division attacked where and when. It also describes the action and any notable incidents, including the actions of the men who were awarded the Victoria Cross.

The maps are annotated trench maps – the same maps the men used to navigate in 1916. The terrain today is very much the same as it was a century ago; minus the trenches, the shell-holes and the general devastation. After the war, most of the roads and villages were all rebuilt in the same place while woods were replanted on the same ground. A modern map bears such a resemblance to the 1916 trench maps that it is possible to navigate with them.

The maps show the trenches before an attack with solid lines. The area captured in the first attack is denoted by a line of dots and the area captured in subsequent attacks is denoted by a line of diamonds. Ground taken but not held is denoted by a line of dashes and dots. Arrows indicate the direction of the attack, both successful and unsuccessful. The division and (where appropriate) brigade numbers are placed to show where they were deployed.

The orders of battle list each division and their General Officer Commanding; they then detail the infantry brigades and battalions. The combination of the information will enable you to locate the battalion you are interested in. Battalion details have not been included because they were moved across the brigade area. The pioneer battalions have been listed because they played an important role in consolidating and fortifying positions across the division's front. The divisional artillery brigades have also been included because of the huge part the gunners played in the battles (around a quarter of soldiers engaged were serving with the Royal Artillery). But it is impossible to locate batteries and brigades because they were usually sited several kilometres behind the front line. It would be very difficult to locate a heavy artillery battery without referring to the unit war diary because they were moved individually.

This book locates where infantry battalions and artillery brigades were engaged – the most important part of many a soldier's story. Anyone wishing to take their research further by following a soldier's movements behind the line should look for Ray Westlake's *British Battalions on the Somme* (Pen & Sword, 1997). It follows the movements of over 600 battalions before, during and after their participation in the fighting, listing billets and villages where they stayed as well as where they fought.

How to Use This Book

Apart from the book, you will need something to help you identify north, the direction all trench maps are orientated: either a compass, a Global Positioning System unit (GPS) used for navigating in the car, or a compass application on your phone.

1. Locate the infantry battalion or artillery brigade in the relevant index.
2. Find the appropriate page with the narrative and read it while consulting the map.
3. Drive to your chosen viewpoint.
4. With the help of landmarks, orientate yourself to face north.
5. The narrative, map and your location all now line up and you are ready to study the battlefield.
6. Drive to the next viewpoint and orientate yourself again to get another view.

Some regular visitors to the Western Front use LinesMan, which is available from the website, www.greatwardigital.com/. This system provides digital trench maps which track your movements on an Iphone or an Ipad. It means you can see all the trenches in your immediate area on your hand-held device.

Planning the Offensive

On 16 May 1916, General Haig's British General Headquarters (GHQ) confirmed there would be an attack on the Somme on 29 June. On 11 June General Joffre wanted the date brought forward to 25 June but a compromise was agreed for the bombardment to start on 24 June with the assault five days later. Rawlinson wanted zero hour at 7am but Foch wanted 9am, so it was set at 7.30am.

The original plan was to advance to a line between Serre, Pozières and Montauban, followed by an advance to Ginchy and Guillemont. It was later extended, with the left on Miraumont and Martinpuich and the right on Ginchy and Flers. The cavalry would advance to Bapaume and then head north, behind the German line.

The Bombardment

Fourth Army had one field gun every 21 metres of front and one heavy gun every 57 metres along its 25,000 metre front. It had 1,010 field artillery pieces, 507 heavy artillery pieces (467 British and 40 French). It also had 288 medium and 28 heavy trench mortars. Over 1.73 million rounds would be fired but less than one in three were heavy calibre shells.

The artillery had two days to register their guns and three to destroy their targets, ready for the infantry assault on day six. Each corps formed a Heavy Artillery Group to deal with targets located by ground and aerial observers. The heavy guns hit trenches, strongpoints and machine gun posts during the day and roads and billets at night. The field guns and trench mortars fired on villages and woods, the front trenches and the wire. Wire cutting operations by the field guns and 2-inch mortars covered all five days. But in many cases the shells were not heavy enough to destroy the targets and far too many shells were duds.

The bombardment was carried out in eighty-minute stints, with forty-minute breaks to allow the guns to cool down. The final bombardment would be sixty-five minutes long, to fool the Germans, and it would end with a short, intense barrage.

Heavy rainstorms delayed the registration of long range targets until the evening of 24 June; but field artillery started firing at the wire and trenches. The heavy artillery registered over 100 batteries the following day. There were showers on 26 June but the destructive bombardment lasted until 3.30pm, when observation planes assessed the damage. Mist and heavy showers prevented aerial observation the following day.

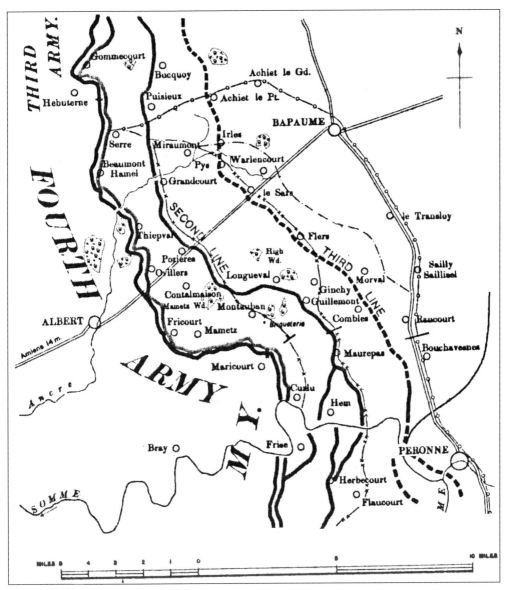

Fourth Army's front, north of the River Somme.

Two extra days of shelling were introduced due to a poor weather forecast, moving the attack forward to 1 July, but Fourth Army had to economise on its heavy calibre ammunition. The weather eventually cleared up on 29 June and the final barrages were doubled in intensity.

The Infantry Preparations
Gas and smoke were released at random intervals in order to encourage the German artillery to open fire and reveal their location. Raids were carried out but only a few prisoners were taken and inspections on the state of the

enemy wire showed that the damage was varied. The Germans were getting more alert as the days passed, waiting for the attack to begin.

30 June was spent marching to the front. The assault troops dumped their greatcoats and packs, before heading into the trenches loaded with equipment and ammunition. The first troops reached their assembly positions around 2am and the final troops were in place by 5.15am. Gaps were opened in the British wire and jumping off tapes laid out. Across no man's land the Germans waited, huddled in their deep dugouts, tired, hungry and anxious, but alive.

The final barrage opened at 6.25am on 1 July and an hour later thousands of men left their trenches and lay down by the jumping off tapes. Others waited to climb over the parapet. At 7.30am the guns lifted their range and the waves of infantry began the walk across no man's land. Rawlinson had told his corps commanders, 'nothing could exist at the conclusion of the bombardment.' Their men were about to find out if it was true.

The Supporting Barrage

Starting at zero hour, the artillery batteries began lengthening their range, according to the pre-arranged barrage program. Batteries were not allowed to switch targets until after midday unless the order came from high authority. The artillery timetable dictated the speed of the advance and the infantry had to halt if they closed up with the barrage. But artillery officers were not allowed to accompany the infantry and ground observers were often too far away to see anything.

Half the heavy guns on VII Corps front lifted to the next trench line at zero hour while half hit the inside flanks of the first objective. In VIII Corps sector there had been arguments over the detonation of the mine under Hawthorn Redoubt. Lieutenant General Sir Aylmer Hunter-Weston wanted it to be detonated four hours before zero but the Inspector of Mines recommended doing it at zero hour. The compromise was to blow it at zero minus ten minutes and all VIII Corps heavy artillery would extend their range at the same time. Five minutes later the howitzers lifted and two minutes later half of 29th Division's field artillery lifted 'to avoid a pause at zero', giving the Germans time to man their parapet.

Both X Corps and III Corps guns had to extend their range by nearly two miles in less than two hours. The heavy artillery jumped from trench to trench while the divisional artillery would 'rake back gradually'. The XV and XIII Corps artillery orders said the field artillery had to 'search back by increasing their range'; or 'gradually drift forward, leaving certain lines at certain hours' or 'creep back by short lifts'. While a planned creeping barrage was in the future, the gunners were attempting to cover the infantry advance.

1 July, VII Corps

Third Army's assault on the Gommecourt salient was a diversionary attack designed to stop the Germans moving reserves south to Fourth Army's front.

46th (North Midland) Division, north of Gommecourt
Viewpoint A: Gommecourt Wood New Cemetery

The men were exhausted after ten days of digging assembly trenches. 1/7th and 1/5th Sherwood Foresters and 1/6th South Staffords and 1/6th North Staffords advanced through the smoke screen, the only time one was used on 1 July. But it had not gone far enough and they emerged from it in front of the wire. Only a few reached the enemy trenches. A wounded Captain John Green was killed rescuing a fellow officer of the 1/5th Sherwoods; he was awarded the Victoria Cross. Shortly after midnight the 1/5th Lincolns entered no man's land and found that the wire had been repaired. The Germans lit up the area and the Lincolns withdrew. Major General the Hon Edward Montagu-Stuart-Wortley was relieved a few days later.

46th (North Midland) Division, Major General the Hon Edward
  Montagu-Stuart-Wortley
137 Brigade, 1/5th and 1/6th South Staffords, 1/5th and 1/6th North
  Staffords
138 Brigade, 1/4th and 1/5th Lincolns, 1/4th and 1/5th Leicesters
139 Brigade, 1/5th, 1/6th, 1/7th and 1/8th Sherwoods
Pioneers, 1st Monmouths: Artillery, CCXXX, CCXXXI, CCXXXII
  and CCXXXIII Brigades

Memorial A: The 46th (North Midland) Division's plaque is in Gommecourt Wood New Cemetery.

56th (1st London) Division, south of Gommecourt
Viewpoint B: Gommecourt British Cemetery No 2

Smoke covering the left flank was thicker than in previous days and it alerted the Germans. Many were shot down negotiating the wire but the survivors charged, shouting 'London Leads!' The 1/5th Londons crossed the trenches east of Gommecourt Wood but the Germans emerged from their dugouts and shot into their backs. The 1/9th Londons crossed three trench

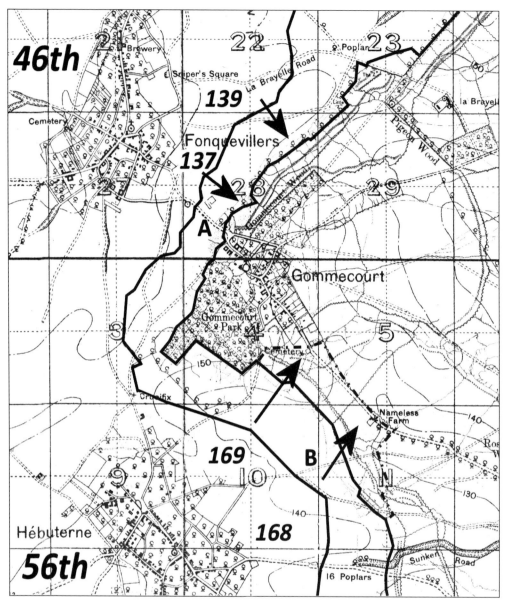

1 July, VII Corps: While 46th Division could not breach the German lines north-west of Gommecourt, 56th Division held a temporary foothold to the south-east.

lines but the bombers sent to capture the Quadrilateral were cut down. Only a few of the 1/12th Londons crossed no man's land and advanced past Nameless Farm; they were never seen again. The 1/14th Londons' left crossed three trenches but eventually withdrew. The right veered into uncut wire and was shot down.

German bombers counter-attacked as artillery fire hit the Londons' reinforcements in no man's land. The two 1/2nd London companies ordered forward around 2pm did not made it across. The survivors were forced back and withdrew when it was dark.

56th (1st London) Division, Major General Charles Hull

167 Brigade, 1/1st London, 1/3rd London, 1/7th and 1/8th Middlesex

168 Brigade, 1/4th, 1/12th, 1/13th and 1/14th London

169 Brigade, 1/2nd, 1/5th, 1/9th and 1/16th London

Pioneers, 1/5th Cheshires: Artillery, CCLXXX, CCLXXXI, CCLXXXII and CCLXXXIII Brigades

1 July, VIII Corps' Left

31st Division, Serre
Viewpoint A: Sheffield Memorial Park

The 12th York and Lancasters, the 11th East Lancashires, and the 13th and 14th York and Lancasters were shot down in no man's land and the few who entered the German trenches were never seen again. The 15th and 16th West Yorkshires were also stopped in no man's land. A few of the 18th Durhams crossed the German line but the 18th West Yorkshires did not get far. The attack was over by noon.

> 31st Division, Major General Robert Wanless O'Gowan
> 92 Brigade, 10th, 11th, 12th and 13th East Yorkshires
> 93 Brigade, 15th, 16th and 18th West Yorkshires, 18th Durhams
> 94 Brigade, 11th East Lancashires, 12th, 13th and 14th York & Lancasters
> Pioneers, 12th KOYLIs: Artillery, CLV, CLXI, CLXIV and CLXVIII Brigades

Memorial A: The Sheffield Memorial Park has traces of trenches and memorials to, amongst others, the Sheffield and Accrington Pals. There is a Sheffield City Battalion memorial in Serre and a Bradford Pals memorial on Hébuterne Church.

4th Division, Redan Ridge
Viewpoint B: Serre Road Number 2 Cemetery and the Quadrilateral
Viewpoint C: Redan Ridge Cemetery Number 1

The 1/8th Warwicks' left was pinned down but the right advanced with the 1st Rifle Brigade. A German mine detonated under Quadrilateral Redoubt did little damage but the few Riflemen who reached Beaumont Trench never returned. Only a few 1st East Lancashires entered the trenches south of Ridge Redoubt. The 1/6th Warwicks carried the 1/8th Warwicks forward to Beaumont Trench. The 1st Somersets veered across the Quadrilateral, avoiding Redan Ridge's machine guns, but the 1st Hampshires were pinned down.

The 1st King's Own, the 2nd Essex and half of the 2nd Lancashire Fusiliers were supposed to wait; but they advanced and were shot down. Drummer Walter Ritchie sounded the charge, rallying the 2nd Seaforths, and later carried messages across no man's land; he was awarded the

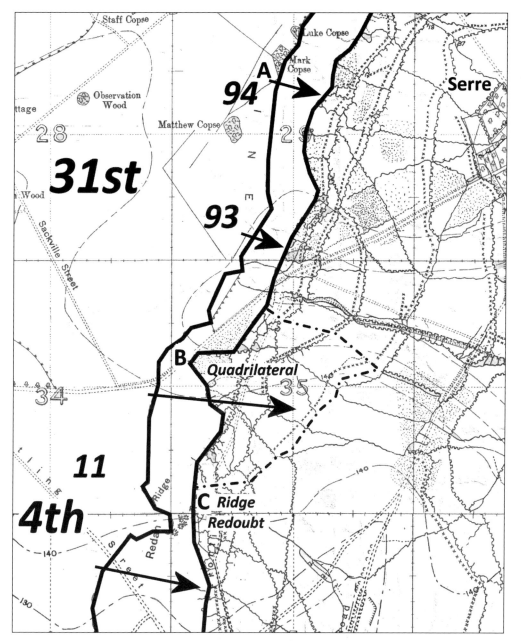

1 July, VIII Corps Left: the 31st Division was cut down in front of the trenches protecting Serre while the 4th Division held a foothold around the Quadrilateral.

Victoria Cross. Only a few 2nd Dublin Fusiliers reached Munich Trench. German counter-attacks recaptured Munich Trench around 11am. Parts of the 2nd Lancashire Fusiliers, 2nd Duke's and 1st Irish Fusiliers reinforced the Quadrilateral but it had to be abandoned the following morning.

4th Division, Major General the Hon William Lambton

10 Brigade, 1st Warwicks, 2nd Seaforths, 1st Irish Fusiliers, 2nd Dublin Fusiliers

11 Brigade, 1st Somersets, 1st East Lancashires, 1st Hampshires, 1st Rifle Brigade

12 Brigade, 1st King's Own, 2nd Lancashire Fusiliers, 2nd Essex, 2nd Duke's

Pioneers, 21st West Yorkshires: Artillery, XIV, XXIX and XXXII Brigades

Memorial B: Serre Road Number 2 Cemetery is the largest on the Somme battlefield with 7,127 burials, most dating from 1916. This concentration cemetery was begun in the spring of 1917 and the rest of the bodies were moved here following the Armistice and for many years afterwards.

Serre Road Number 2 Cemetery is the largest British cemetery on the Somme battlefield.

1 July, VIII Corps' Right

29th Division, Beaumont Hamel and Y-Ravine
Viewpoint A: The Argylls memorial next to the Sunken Road
Viewpoint B: Hawthorn Ridge Craters
Viewpoint C: Newfoundland Park

A mine was blown under Hawthorn Ridge Redoubt at 7.20am and two 2nd Royal Fusiliers platoons reached the near side of the crater. The 1st Lancashire Fusiliers were shot down around the sunken lane in no man's land and only a few 2nd Royal Fusiliers reached the mine crater. The 1st Dublin Fusiliers and 16th Middlesex were hit by artillery before they entered no man's land and then stopped by the Bergwerk's machine guns.

The 2nd SWBs and 1st Inniskillings were shot down by machine guns covering Y-Ravine and only a few made it to the front trench. The 1st KOSBs and the 1st Borders wanted a new bombardment but white flares were seen and reported as British troops on the first objective; they were German flares reporting something else. The two battalions were cut down by artillery and machine gun fire.

Two more battalions were sent forward and the 1st Newfoundland Regiment left the congested trenches and moved forward alone at 9.05am. Only a handful reached the German trench and very few returned. The 1st Essex pushed through the equally congested trenches, which were largely under direct German observation, and advanced later with the same result. Although there were plans to make more attacks, they were not carried out.

> 29th Division, Major General Aylmer Hunter-Weston
> 86 Brigade, 2nd Royal Fusiliers, 1st Lancashire Fusiliers, 16th Middlesex, 1st Dublin Fusiliers
> 87 Brigade, 2nd South Wales Borderers, 1st KOSBs, 1st Inniskilling Fusiliers, 1st Borders
> 88 Brigade, 4th Worcesters, 1st Essex, 2nd Hampshires, 1st Newfoundland
> Pioneers, 2nd Monmouths: Artillery, XV (RHA), XVII, CXXXII and CXLVII Brigades

Memorial A: The Argylls memorial overlooks the Sunken Lane. The 1/8th Argylls attacked towards Beaumont Hamel on 13 November.

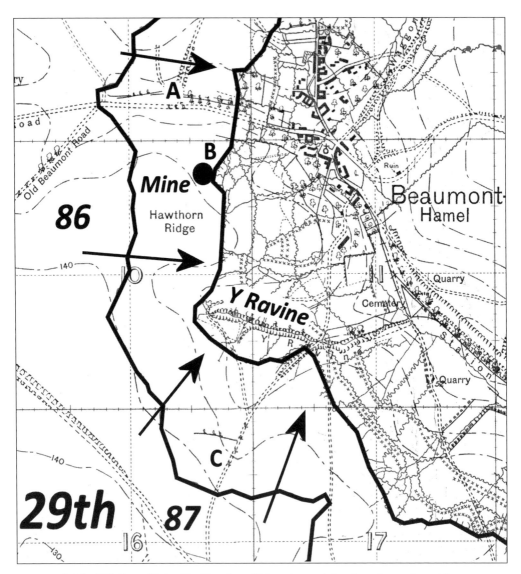

1 July, VIII Corps Right: The Hawthorn Ridge mine and the alteration to the artillery barrage compromised the 29th Division's attack on Beaumont Hamel.

Memorial B: There are two craters on Hawthorn Ridge. The first was blown on 1 July and the second on 13 November. They can be visited but with great care, as the craters are full of trees and undergrowth.

Memorial C: The Newfoundland Memorial Park covers the site of the Regiment's advance on 1 July, when 686 out of 810 men who went over the top were killed, wounded or captured. The divisional commander later commented: 'It was a magnificent display of trained and disciplined valour, and its assault failed of success because dead men can advance no further'. There are preserved trenches, a number of cemeteries, memorials to the 29th Division and the 51st Division, and the Newfoundland Caribou memorial. While the British troops started near the road, the German position was based around Y-Ravine, at the far end of the park; Canadian guides are on call to assist visitors. There is also a Visitor Centre with toilets, and a useful map.

The Hawthorn Ridge mine explodes.

1 and 2 July, X Corps' Left

36th (Ulster) Division, Schwaben Redoubt
Viewpoint A: Helen's Tower and the Pope's Nose
Viewpoint B: Thiepval civilian cemetery

Private Billy McFadzean of the 14th Irish Rifles was killed in the assembly trench waiting for zero hour when he lay on top of two grenades that had lost their pins; he was posthumously awarded the Victoria Cross.

North of the Ancre the 12th Irish Rifles and 9th Irish Fusiliers were shot down in no man's land. One hundred 12th Irish Rifles tried again at 10.12am but they did not get far. Private Robert Quigg rescued wounded of the 12th Irish Rifles and Lieutenant Geoffrey Cather rescued wounded of the 9th Irish Fusiliers. Quigg survived but Cather was killed; they were both awarded the Victoria Cross.

Few 13th and 11th Irish Rifles reached the Hansa Line south of the Ancre. The 10th and 9th Inniskillings overran the German trenches and crossed Schwaben Redoubt. Captain Eric Bell silenced a machine gun but was killed rallying groups of men; he was posthumously awarded the Victoria Cross.

A few Ulstermen reached the Grandcourt Line and Stuff Redoubt and they were joined by most of 109 Brigade. But they had been forced back into Schwaben Redoubt by mid-afternoon. During the evening the 9th Irish Rifles carried supplies across no man's land.

> 36th (Ulster) Division, Major General Oliver Nugent
> 107 Brigade, 8th, 9th, 10th and 15th Irish Rifles
> 108 Brigade, 9th Irish Fusiliers, 11th, 12th and 13th Irish Rifles
> 109 Brigade, 9th, 10th and 11th Inniskilling Fusiliers, 14th Irish
>   Rifles
> Pioneers, 16th Irish Rifles: Artillery, CLIII, CLIV, CLXXII and
>   CLXXIII Brigades

Memorial A: The Ulster Tower is a replica of Helen's Tower, near Bangor, in County Down; it is a memorial to the men of the 36th (Ulster) Division. There is a small museum and café next to the tower, staffed by members of the Somme Association, and guided visits to Thiepval Wood are sometimes available. There are memorials to the division's VC winners and members of the Orange Order in the grounds.

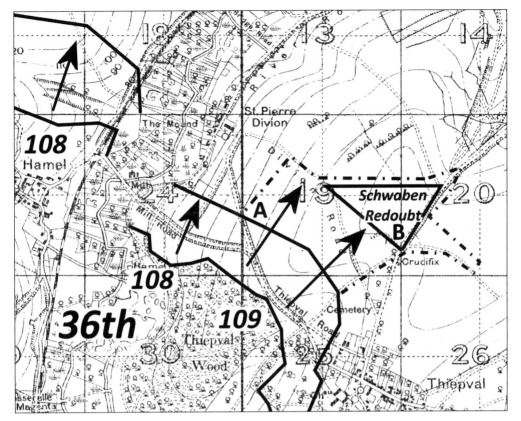

1 July, X Corps Left: 36th Division was pinned down astride the River Ancre but initially advanced across the Schwaben Redoubt, north of Thiepval.

49th (West Riding) Division in Reserve

At 11.30am the 1/6th West Yorkshires and part of the 1/8th West Yorkshires were shot down advancing on Thiepval. During the evening the 1/7th and 1/5th West Yorks and part of the 1/8th West Yorks joined the Ulstermen. Corporal George Sanders and thirty 1/7th West Yorks were left behind in Schwaben Redoubt when the rest withdrew. They fought on for thirty-six hours and Sanders was awarded the Victoria Cross.

    49th (West Riding) Division, Major General Edward Perceval
    146 Brigade, 1/5th, 1/6th, 1/7th and 1/8th West Yorks
    147 Brigade, 1/4th, 1/5th, 1/6th and 1/7th Duke's
    148 Brigade, 1/4th and 1/5th KOYLIs, 1/4th and 1/5th York & Lancasters
    Pioneers, 3rd Monmouths: Artillery, CCXLV, CCXLVI, CCXLVII and CCXLVIII Brigades

1 and 2 July, X Corps' Right

32nd Division, Thiepval

Viewpoint A: 18th Division's memorial, Thiepval village
Viewpoint B: Leipzig Salient

The 15th and 16th Lancashire Fusiliers and 16th HLI were shot down between Thiepval Wood and the village. The message came back, only 'bulletproof soldiers could have taken Thiepval'. The 17th HLI rushed Leipzig Salient but the Wonder Work's machine guns stopped them going further and the bombers could not clear Hindenburg or Lemberg Trench. Sergeant James Turnbull fought on until he was killed and he was posthumously awarded the Victoria Cross. The 11th Borders (the Lonsdales) in Authuille Wood were unaware the attack had failed and only a few made it to Leipzig Redoubt when they advanced at 8.30am.

There were reports of British troops in Thiepval, so the artillery stopped firing on the village. At 8.45am parts of the 1st Dorsets and 19th Lancashire Fusiliers left Thiepval Wood but few reached Leipzig Redoubt. Thirty minutes later, part of the 16th Lancashire Fusiliers advanced from Johnson's

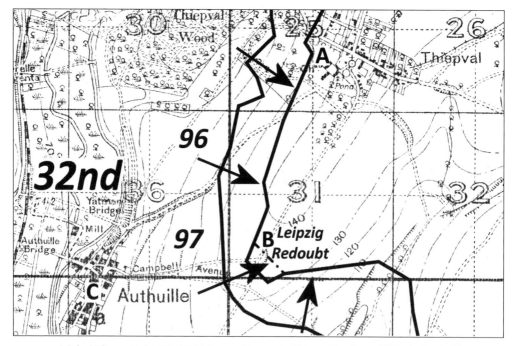

1 July, X Corps Right: 32nd Division could not take Thiepval but it established a foothold in Leipzig Redoubt.

Post at the east corner of Thiepval Wood; no one made it across no man's land. At 1.30pm part of the 2nd Inniskillings failed to advance from Thiepval Wood to Thiepval. Part of the 2nd Manchesters left Leipzig Salient but no one reached Hindenburg Trench.

On 2 July, zero hour for a new attack was postponed for three hours because the troops could not get into position. But no one told the artillery and the batteries fired as planned, leaving them short of ammunition for the new time. The 2nd South Lancashires were stopped by wire and the 8th Borders captured the first trench but soon had to withdraw. The 11th Cheshires were 'mowed down, line after line' and the 15th HLI failed to capture Hindenburg Trench.

32nd Division, Major General William Rycroft
14 Brigade, 19th Lancashire Fusiliers, 1st Dorsets, 2nd Manchesters,
     15th HLI
96 Brigade, 16th North'd Fusiliers, 15th and 16th Lancashire
     Fusiliers, 2nd Inniskillings
97 Brigade, 11th Borders, 2nd KOYLIs, 16th and 17th HLI
Pioneers, 17th Northumberland Fusiliers: Artillery, CLV, CLXI,
     CLXIV, CLXVIII Brigades

Memorial C: The 15th, 16th and 17th Lancashire Fusiliers (Salford Pals) memorial is in Authuille and the 15th, 16th and 17th HLI (Glasgow Pals battalions) have theirs on the wall of Authuille church.

The Ulster Tower remembers the men of 36th (Ulster) Division.

1 July, III Corps' Left

8th Division, Ovillers

Viewpoint A: Authuille road north from Ovillers, turn right, stop at the end after 200 metres
Viewpoint B: Ovillers Military Cemetery

The advancing infantry would be under fire from the Leipzig Salient to the north and from La Boisselle to the south. The divisional general, Major General Hudson, had wanted the high ground either side of his objective captured before his men left their trenches but Rawlinson rejected his proposal.

The leading waves of the 8th KOYLIs and part of the 8th York and Lancasters crossed three German trenches but the rest became casualties in no man's land. The 9th York and Lancasters and 11th Sherwoods were also halted when they advanced. A group of bombers were also stopped from advancing along a sunken lane from the Nab. However, they all held on until the 2nd Lincolns fell back on their right and they too withdrew.

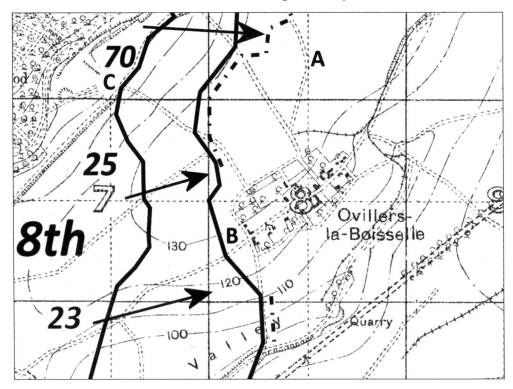

1 July, III Corps Left: 8th Division failed to clear the trenches covering Ovillers.

Only a few of the 2nd Berkshires, 2nd Lincolns and 1st Irish Rifles reached the German trenches. The survivors eventually gathered in the forward German trench under Lieutenant Colonel Bastard of the 2nd Lincolns. The 2nd Rifle Brigade had been ordered to hold the British front line. The 2nd Middlesex and 2nd Devons later made a second attempt to get across but only a few made it across no man's land. Half the 2nd West Yorkshires also advanced, only to be pinned down. The 2nd Scottish Rifles were held back, preventing further loss of life. Colonel Bastard went back to collect reinforcements, only to be told no more men would be sent forward, so he returned to organise a withdrawal. The survivors crept back during the night.

8th Division, Major General Havelock Hudson

23 Brigade, 2nd Devons, 2nd West Yorkshires, 2nd Middlesex, 2nd Scottish Rifles

24 Brigade, 1st Worcesters, 1st Sherwoods, 2nd Northants, 2nd East Lancashires

25 Brigade, 2nd Lincolns, 2nd Berkshires, 1st Irish Rifles, 2nd Rifle Brigade

Pioneers, 22nd Durhams: Artillery, V (RHA) Brigade, XXXIII, and XLV Brigades

Memorial C: Ulverston Trench is at the north-east corner of Blighty Wood, north of Ovillers.

Lochnagar Crater was created when a huge mine exploded on 34th Division's front on 1 July.

1 July, III Corps' Right

34th Division, La Boisselle
Viewpoint A: La Boisselle civilian cemetery
Viewpoint B: Gordon Dump Cemetery
Viewpoint C: Lochnagar Crater

A 40,000lb mine (nearly 18 tons) detonated under Y Sap at 7.28am, but the 20th, 23rd and 25th Northumberland Fusiliers were shot down as they advanced up Mash Valley. A second 60,000lb mine (nearly 27 tons) simultaneously destroyed Schwaben Höhe, and the 21st, 22nd and 26th Northumberland Fusiliers overran the first three trenches. A few reached Bailiff Wood but most were killed or taken prisoner. The rest were soon pushed back to the first trench.

The 10th Lincolns and 11th Suffolks advanced at 7.35am 'as [if] on parade and never flinched'. But the 'men were soon spun round and dropping everywhere,' shot down by fire from Bloater Trench and Sausage Redoubt. The 24th Northumberland Fusiliers were ordered to stand fast but some had already moved off. Few crossed no man's land but a handful reached Contalmaison.

The 15th Royal Scots advanced at 7.30am and overran Kipper Trench; the 16th Royal Scots veered right but the 27th Northumberland Fusiliers were pinned down in no man's land. The 16th Royal Scots held Round Wood and the 15th Royal Scots held Birch Tree Wood and Shelter Wood. The survivors cleared Scots Redoubt and Wood Alley.

By 10.00am 34th Division's attack was over. No one had crossed Mash Valley; a few were holding the Schwaben Höhe crater; no one had crossed Sausage Valley and some were on the wrong side of the Fricourt spur around Round Wood and Birch Tree Wood.

> 34th Division, Major General Edward Ingouville-Williams
> 101 Brigade, 15th and 16th Royal Scots, 10th Lincolns, 11th Suffolks
> 102 (Tyneside Scottish) Brigade, 20th, 21st, 22nd and 23rd Northumberland Fusiliers
> 103 (Tyneside Irish) Brigade, 24th, 25th, 26th and 27th Northumberland Fusiliers
> Pioneers, 18th North'd Fusiliers: Artillery, CLII, CLX, CLXXV and CLXXVI Brigades

Memorial C: At 7.28am on 1 July 60,000lbs of explosives detonated south of La Boisselle, creating Lochnagar Crater. A Briton, Richard Dunning, purchased the crater in 1978 and ceremonies are held every 1 July and 11 November.

Memorial D: The tunnels beneath the Glory Hole crater field have been subject to detailed underground exploration in recent years.

Memorial E: The Tyneside Scottish and Irish Brigades memorial is at the west end of La Boisselle.

Memorial F: The 34th Division memorial is at the east end of La Boisselle.

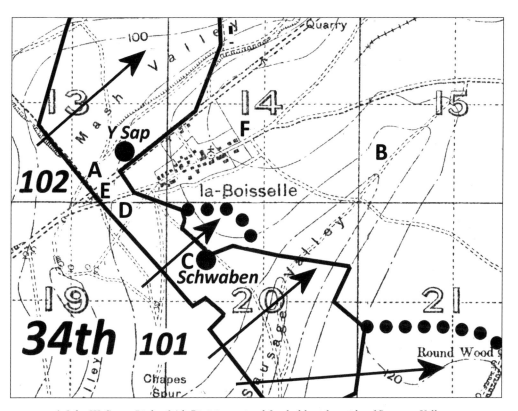

1 July, III Corps Right: 34th Division gained footholds either side of Sausage Valley.

1 July, XV Corps' Left

21st Division, North of Fricourt
Viewpoint A: Rue de la Boisselle, hard-standing by fork in the road
Viewpoint B: Tambour craters
Viewpoint C: Fricourt German Cemetery

The 10th and 9th KOYLIs advanced from South Sausage Trench and across Sausage Valley and reached the German support trench. The 1st East Yorkshires and 15th Durhams followed and reached the Sunken Road, north of Fricourt. The 1st Lincolns and 10th Green Howards then reinforced the front line. The 8th Somersets crossed Empress Trench and advanced past the north side of Fricourt and 150 of the 4th Middlesex reached the Sunken Road. At 8.40am the 8th Lincolns and the 10th York and Lancasters crossed no man's land. Lozenge Alley and Crucifix Trench were taken but Fricourt Farm remained in German hands.

Three mines exploded in the Tambour crater field at 7.28am. Two minutes later the 10th West Yorks advanced across Köenig Trench. A wounded Major Stewart Loudoun-Shand cheered his men on until he died; he was posthumously awarded the Victoria Cross. The West Yorkshires headed towards Red Cottage, at the north-west corner of Fricourt, where the majority of them were eventually overrun.

The advance towards Fricourt Farm and Shelter Wood resumed at 2.30pm. The 15th Durhams and the 10th KOYLIs advanced from Crucifix Trench ten minutes after the barrage had lifted but they did not get far. Machine guns in Fricourt Farm and Fricourt Wood stopped the advance from Lonely Trench and Lozenge Wood. The 7th Green Howards were shot down between the Tambour craters and Wing Corner, at the south end of Fricourt. Around 4.30pm a flank was formed along Crucifix Trench and Lozenge Alley, facing Fricourt. The 12th and 13th Northumberland Fusiliers then moved forward to take it over.

21st Division, Major General David Campbell
62 Brigade, 12th North'd Fusiliers, 13th North'd Fusiliers, 1st Lincolns, 10th Green Howards
63 Brigade, 8th Lincolns, 8th Somersets, 12th Green Howards, 10th York and Lancasters
64 Brigade, 9th KOYLIs, 10th KOYLIs, 14th Durhams, 15th Durhams

Pioneers, 14th North'd Fusiliers: Artillery, XCIV, XCV, XCVI and
   XCVII Brigade
Attached from 17th (Northern) Division
50 Brigade, 10th West Yorkshires, 7th East Yorkshires, 7th Green
   Howards, 6th Dorsets

*Memorial B: Three mines were set to detonate in the Tambour (Drum)
crater field on 1 July, but only two were fired.*

*Memorial C: There are 280 military cemeteries in the Somme Department
but the only German cemetery stands alongside the Sunken Lane, north of
Fricourt. There are 17,000 burials; and the rows of grey crosses and the
huge mass grave in Fricourt German Cemetery are a sombre contrast to
the white headstones of a Commonwealth War Graves Cemetery.*

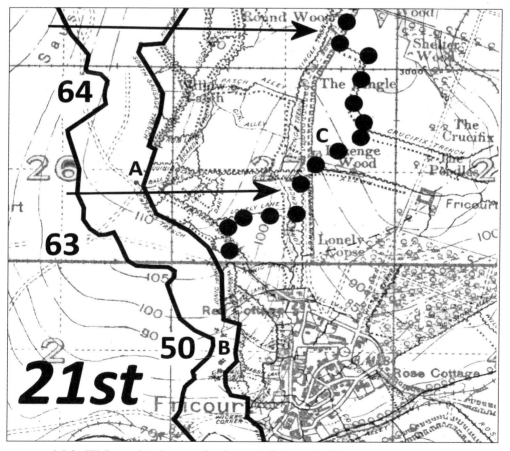

1 July, XV Corps: 21st Division faced a tough fight north of Fricourt

1 July, XV Corps' Right

Viewpoint A: Devonshire Cemetery
Viewpoint B: The Shrine, Mametz civilian cemetery
Viewpoint C: Dantzig Alley Cemetery

7th Division, Mametz

The division's right flank advanced at 7.30am, north-east of Fricourt Wood, and the left flank would follow through the village and wood at 2.30pm. Four small mines detonated at zero hour and the 2nd Borders overran the front line before wheeling left over Quarry Spur. They then crossed Apple Valley and Hidden Lane before entering Hidden Wood. The 9th Devons clambered down a steep slope and suffered heavy casualties before they reached Mansell Copse. They stopped in the second trench because they had lost all their officers. The 2nd Gordons' left were stopped by wire but a small mine allowed the right company to reach Shrine Alley before they too were stopped. The 8th Devons then filled the gap between the Gordons and the 9th Devons.

A mine destroyed Bulgar Point, allowing the 1st South Staffords to cross Cemetery Trench and enter Mametz as the 22nd Manchesters captured Bucket Trench. The 21st Manchesters could not advance beyond Cemetery Trench and the 2nd Queen's could not reach Dantzig Alley. There was another short bombardment but Dantzig Alley was still not taken. A third bombardment allowed the 2nd Warwicks, 1st South Staffords and 21st Manchesters to clear Mametz as the 2nd Queen's captured Dantzig Alley.

The second phase of the attack began when the 20th Manchesters and 1st Welsh Fusiliers advanced from the Maricourt spur, south of Fricourt, at 2.30pm. Movement in the open was impossible but the Welsh Fusiliers' bombers cleared Sunken Road Trench and Rectangle.

At 3.30pm the 8th Devons advanced past the Shrine to Dantzig Trench, allowing the 9th Devons to capture Bunny Trench. The 2nd Queen's reached Fritz Trench north-east of Mametz by 6.30pm and an hour later it was joined by the 1st South Staffords. The Mametz area was clear by evening.

7th Division, Major General Herbert Watts
20 Brigade, 8th Devons, 9th Devons, 2nd Borders, 2nd Gordons
22 Brigade, 2nd Warwicks, 2nd Irish Regiment, 1st Welsh
    Fusiliers, 20th Manchesters
91 Brigade, 2nd Queen's, 1st South Staffords, 21st Manchesters,
    22nd Manchesters

Pioneers, 24th Manchesters: Artillery, XIV (RHA), XXII and
  XXXV Brigades

*Memorial A: On 1 July the 8th and 9th Devons buried their dead in the
Devonshire Cemetery in Mansell Copse. They erected a sign stating, 'The
Devonshires held this trench, the Devonshires hold it still'. A stone memorial
with the same words was unveiled in 1986.*

*Memorial D: The four Manchester Pals Battalions are remembered by a
memorial in Mametz village.*

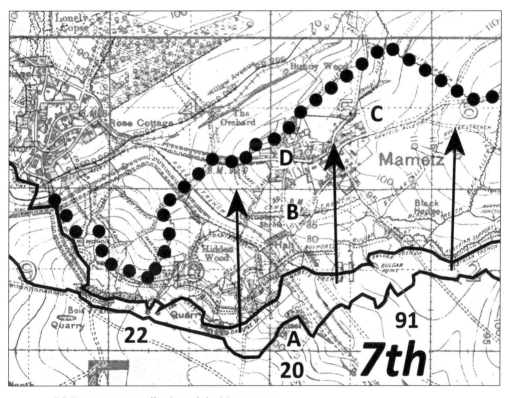

7th Division eventually cleared the Mametz area.

1 July, XIII Corps' Left

18th Division, North of Carnoy
Viewpoint A: Hard-standing between Carnoy and Montauban
Viewpoint B: Pull-in on the Mametz road, west of Montauban

A small mine detonated on the left flank at 7.27am and the 11th Royal Fusiliers and 7th Bedfords advanced across Austrian Trench to Emden Trench. The Fusiliers moved astride Black Alley whilst the Bedfords were shot up by the Triangle machine gun. They then cleared Pommiers Trench, with the 10th Essex helping on the right. The Royal Fusiliers cleared Pommiers Redoubt and Beetle Alley, with the 6th Northants' help. They stopped at White Trench, overlooking Caterpillar Valley, having advanced over a mile.

A mine detonated under Casino Point at 7.27am and some of the 6th Berkshires were hit by the debris. Two small mines exploded in front of the 8th Norfolks, while a Livens Flame Projector sprayed burning oil across the Carnoy Road craters. The two battalions advanced across Bay Trench, Mine Trench, Bund and Bund Support Trench. They were stopped by Pommiers Trench and the Loop, where the rest of the 8th Norfolks had been delayed. The 10th Essex also failed to take the Loop but the Norfolks' right cleared the Castle.

The 7th Buffs failed to clear the Carnoy Road craters; so enfilade fire hit the 7th Queen's and 7th Queen's Own. The 8th East Surreys kicked footballs into no man's land but they were pinned down until 30th Division cleared Train Alley. The Queen's then led the 8th East Surreys towards Train Alley.

The 7th Buffs eventually cleared the Carnoy Road craters but the Germans held onto Breslau Support Trench and the Loop. The 7th Queen's Own by-passed the Loop and reached the Montauban road about noon. The Germans then withdrew and the 7th Queen's met the East Surreys and Buffs in Train Alley. The Loop eventually surrendered to the 6th Berkshires, so the 8th Norfolks and 7th Queen's could reach Back Trench. By late afternoon several groups had linked up in Loop Trench.

    18th (Eastern) Division, Major General Ivor Maxse
    53 Brigade, 8th Norfolks, 8th Suffolks, 10th Essex, 6th Berkshires
    54 Brigade, 11th Royal Fusiliers, 7th Bedfords, 8th Northants, 12th
        Middlesex
    55 Brigade, 7th Queen's, 7th Buffs, 8th East Surreys, 7th Queen's Own
    Pioneers, 8th Sussex: Artillery, LXXXII, LXXXIII, LXXXIV and
        LXXXV Brigades

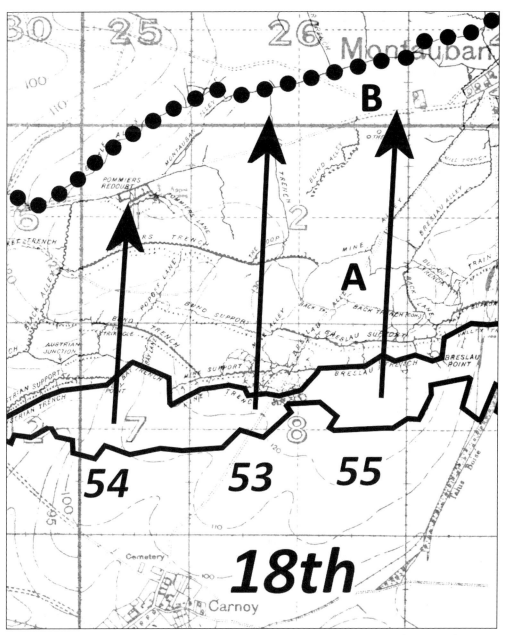

1 July, XIII Corps Left: 18th Division captured all its objectives to the west of Montauban.

1 to 3 July, XIII Corps' Right

30th Division, Montauban

Viewpoint A: Maricourt road, tarmac track by copse in no man's land
Viewpoint B: South side of the village, pull-in at end of sunken lane
Viewpoint C: Crucifix at the north-east corner of Montauban

The 18th King's and 19th Manchesters advanced too fast and had to wait until the barrage had lifted from Alt Trench. Meanwhile, men detailed to mop up caught many Germans in their dugouts. The King's then came under enfilade fire from Train Alley and the Warren, where 18th Division had been held up. The Manchesters found a weak spot in the German line and while the two battalions soon reached Glatz Redoubt, artillery fire stopped the 2nd Green Howards in no man's land.

Lieutenant Colonel Fairfax of the 17th King's and Commandant Le Petit of the 3/153rd Regiment advanced arm-in-arm to celebrate the Allied co-operation. The 20th King's and 17th King's advanced 'as though on parade, in quick time', crossing Favière Trench, Alt Alley and Casement Trench, with the 2nd Bedfords following. Dublin Trench had been obliterated, so the King's had to dig in beyond it.

The 16th and 17th Manchesters moved up to Train Valley, with the 2nd Royal Scots Fusiliers following, and then continued the advance across Southern Trench and passed through Montauban to Montauban Alley, overlooking Caterpillar Valley. The 30th Division had advanced over one mile. Meanwhile, the 20th King's secured La Briqueterie factory on the right flank.

> 30th Division, Major General John Shea
> 21 Brigade, 18th King's Own, 19th Manchesters, 2nd Green
>   Howards, 2nd Wiltshires
> 89 Brigade, 17th King's, 19th King's, 20th King's, 2nd Bedfords
> 90 Brigade, 16th Manchesters, 17th Manchesters, 18th
>   Manchesters, 2nd Scots Fusiliers
> Pioneers, 11th South Lancashires: Artillery, CXLVIII, CXLIX, CL
>   and CLI Brigades

Memorial D: At the south end of the Maricourt–Montauban road is a memorial to Colonel Fairfax's and Commandant Le Petit's advance together, the boundary of the British and French advances.

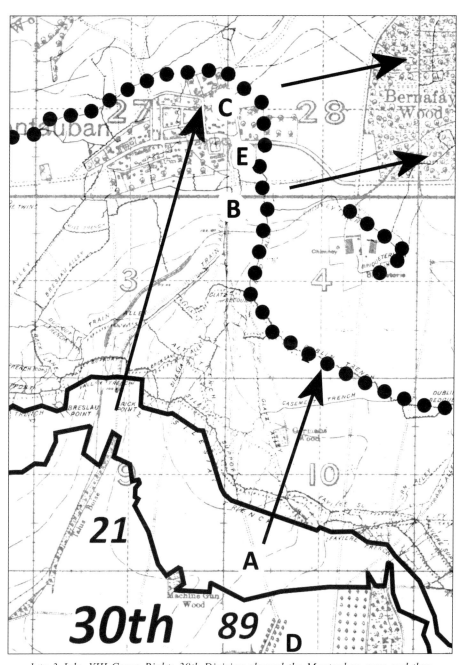

1 to 3 July, XIII Corps Right: 30th Division cleared the Montauban area and then occupied Bernafay Wood.

Memorial E: Four battalions of the King's Regiment (the Liverpool Pals) took part in the capture of Montauban. They are remembered on a memorial at the east end of the village.

9th (Scottish) Division, Bernafay Wood
Viewpoint C: Crucifix, north-east corner of Montauban

The 12th Royal Scots and the 6th KOSBs occupied an abandoned Bernafay Wood at 9pm on 3 July. Montauban Alley was also cleared but the Germans held Trônes Wood.

> 9th (Scottish) Division, Major General William Furse
> 26 Brigade, 8th Black Watch, 7th Seaforths, 5th Camerons, 10th
>   Argylls
> 27 Brigade, 11th and 12th Royal Scots, 6th KOSBs, 9th Scottish
>   Rifles
> South African Brigade, 1st, 2nd, 3rd and 4th South African
>   Regiments
> Pioneers, 9th Seaforths: Artillery, L, LI, LII and LIII Brigades

Troops advancing near Mametz village on 1 July.

2 to 8 July, III Corps

19th (Western) Division, La Boisselle
Viewpoint A: Lochnagar Crater across Sausage Valley
Viewpoint B: Gordon Dump Cemetery

A deep communications trench stopped the 9th Cheshires advancing far from Lochnagar Crater at 4.30am on 2 July. At 3.30pm the 9th Welsh Fusiliers and the 6th Wiltshires captured the Glory Hole craters and the Cheshires advanced into the south side of La Boisselle. The 7th South Lancashires also cleared Sausage Redoubt and 1,000 metres of trench.

At 2.15am on 3 July the 10th Worcesters cleared trenches on the north side of La Boisselle. Private Thomas Turrall fought on when surrounded and then carried a seriously wounded Lieutenant Jennings back to safety; he was awarded the Victoria Cross. The 8th North Staffords and 5th SWBs simultaneously advanced along the south side of the village.

The 8th Gloucesters and 9th Cheshires cleared La Boisselle only to be driven from the east end until reinforced by the 9th Welsh. Lieutenant Colonel Adrian Carton de Wiart of the Gloucesters led the defence; he was awarded the Victoria Cross. The 7th King's Own spent 4 July clearing La Boisselle but the 1st Sherwoods and the 4th Grenadier Guards could not clear the area east of the village. Lieutenant Thomas Wilkinson of the 7th Loyals stopped a counter-attack with a machine gun but he was killed carrying a wounded man to safety; he was posthumously awarded the Victoria Cross. The 7th East Lancashires cleared the area east of La Boisselle on the evening of 6 July.

The artillery barrage failed to move forward east of La Boisselle at 8am on 7 July and it took an hour to coordinate the advance in pouring rain. The attack by the 7th King's Own and the 9th Welsh surprised the Germans and the objective was taken with the 6th Wiltshires help. The 9th Welsh Fusiliers then secured the right flank facing Contalmaison. On the evening of 8 July the 13th Royal Fusiliers advanced 1,000 metres adjacent to the Bapaume road because the Germans had withdrawn to Pozières.

19th (Western) Division, Major General Tom Bridges
56 Brigade, 7th King's Own, 7th East Lancashires, 7th South Lancashires, 7th Loyals
57 Brigade, 10th Warwicks, 8th Gloucesters, 10th Worcesters, 8th North Staffords

58 Brigade, 9th Cheshires, 9th Welsh Fusiliers, 9th Welsh, 6th
  Wiltshires
Pioneers, 5th SWBs: Artillery, LXXXVI, LXXXVII, LXXXVIII
  and LXXXIX Brigades
Attached from 37th Division
111 Brigade, 10th and 13th Royal Fusiliers, 13th KRRC and 13th
  Rifle Brigade

Memorial D: 19th Division memorial is in front of La Boisselle church.

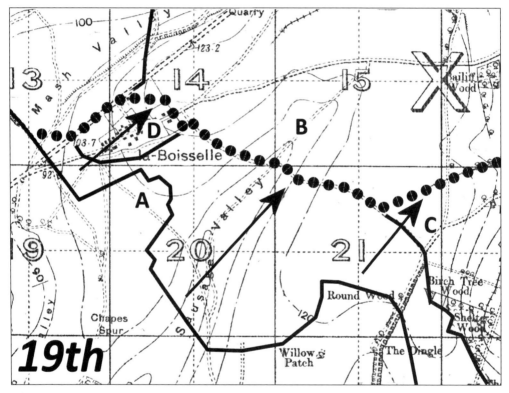

2 July, III Corps: 19th Division fought its way through La Boisselle and cleared Sausage Valley.

2 to 7 July, XV Corps

21st Division, Fricourt Farm
Viewpoint A: Hard-standing beyond Shelter Wood

On 2 July the 10th Green Howards reached the Poodles, north of Fricourt. The 1st Lincolns cleared Shelter Wood and Birch Tree Wood the following morning, helped by the 12th and 13th Northumberland Fusiliers.

> 21st Division, Major General David Campbell
> 62 Brigade, 12th and 13th Northumberland Fusiliers, 1st Lincolns, 10th Green Howards
> 63 Brigade, 8th Lincolns, 8th Somersets, 12th Green Howards, 10th York and Lancasters
> 64 Brigade, 9th and 10th KOYLIs, 14th and 15th Durhams
> Pioneers, 14th Northumberland Fusiliers: Artillery, XCIV, XCV, XCVI and XCVII Brigades

17th (Northern) Division, Fricourt and Railway Alley
Viewpoint B: Hard-standing east of Fricourt
Viewpoint C: Dantzig Alley Cemetery

The 8th South Staffords and 7th Lincolns occupied an abandoned Fricourt on 2 July. The Lincolns then cleared Fricourt Wood, as the 10th Sherwoods and the Staffords cleared a trench between Fricourt Farm and Fricourt Wood. The Sherwoods' bombers cleared part of Railway Alley that evening.

The 7th Borders advanced across Railway Alley at 9am on 3 July but only one company reached Bottom Wood. No one told the artillery of the 8th South Staffords' and 7th Lincolns' next attacks, so their advance took Crucifix Trench by surprise. The 10th Sherwoods later captured Railway Copse and the Staffords cleared Railway Alley. The 10th Lancashire Fusiliers and 9th Northumberland Fusiliers rushed Shelter Alley and Quadrangle Trench at 12.45am on 4 July.

> 17th (Northern) Division, Major General Thomas Pilcher
> 50 Brigade, 10th West Yorkshires, 7th East Yorkshires, 7th Green Howards, 6th Dorsets
> 51 Brigade, 7th Lincolns, 7th Borders, 8th South Staffords, 10th Sherwoods

52 Brigade, 9th North'd Fusiliers, 10th Lancashire Fusiliers, 9th
   Duke's, 12th Manchesters
Pioneers, 7th York and Lancasters: Artillery, LXXVIII, LXXIX,
   LXXX and LXXXI Brigades

*Memorial D: There is a memorial to the 7th Green Howards in Fricourt
British Cemetery.*

7th Division, North of Mametz and Bottom Wood
Viewpoint E: Quadrangle Wood

Early on 2 July, 22 Brigade reached the railway south of Fricourt. The 8th
Devons captured Orchard Trench North and the 2nd Queen's occupied the
Queen's Nullah and White Trench. The 21st Manchesters occupied Bottom
Wood early on 3 July and the 2nd Irish Regiment investigated Mametz
Wood later that night, finding it occupied. At 12.45am on 4 July the 1st

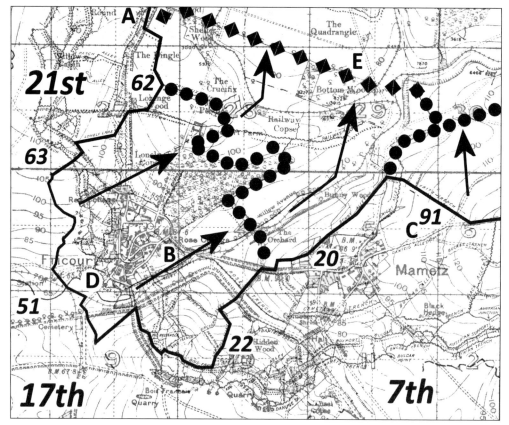

The Germans withdrew from the Fricourt salient as 21st, 17th and 7th Divisions closed in.

Moving out of a trench into no man's land.

Welsh Fusiliers and the 2nd Irish Regiment were shot down approaching Wood Trench and Strip Trench. The poet Second Lieutenant Siegfried Sassoon 'did splendidly' in the bombing fight.

> 7th Division, Major General Herbert Watts
> 20 Brigade, 8th Devons, 9th Devons, 2nd Borders, 2nd Gordons
> 22 Brigade, 2nd Warwicks, 2nd Irish Regiment, 1st Welsh Fusiliers, 20th Manchesters
> 91 Brigade, 2nd Queen's, 1st South Staffords, 21st Manchesters, 22nd Manchesters
> Pioneers, 24th Manchesters: Artillery, XIV (RHA), XXII and XXXV Brigades

2 to 10 July, XIII Corps

30th Division, Trônes Wood
Viewpoint A: Road between Bernafay Wood and Trônes Wood

The 2nd Green Howards were pinned down in front of Trônes Wood at 8am on 8 July. A 2nd Wiltshires' company entered Maltz Horn Trench, while the 19th Manchesters linked up with the French. A second Wiltshires' company entered Trônes Wood at 1pm and was later reinforced by the 18th King's and 19th Manchesters.

The 2nd Scots Fusiliers cleared Maltz Horn Trench at 3am on 9 July. Gas shells delayed the 17th Manchesters for three hours and they found Trônes Wood abandoned. Most withdrew to Bernafay Wood when the Germans counter-attacked at 3pm. Some of the Manchesters and Scots Fusiliers remained at the south end of Trônes Wood.

The 16th Manchesters recaptured the wood early on 10 July, only to be driven out again by 8am. After a day of reorganising, there was another attempt by the 2nd Bedfords and the 20th King's bombers at 3.27am on 11 July. Fighting continued all day but they were driven into the south-east corner, despite reinforcements from the 17th King's.

> 30th Division, Major General John Shea
> 21 Brigade, 18th King's Own, 19th Manchesters, 2nd Green Howards, 2nd Wiltshires
> 89 Brigade, 17th King's, 19th King's, 20th King's, 2nd Bedfords
> 90 Brigade, 16th Manchesters, 17th Manchesters, 18th Manchesters, 2nd Scots Fusiliers
> Pioneers, 11th South Lancashires: Artillery, CXLVIII, CXLIX, CL Brigade and CLI Brigades

18th (Eastern) Division, Trônes Wood
Viewpoint B: The 18th Division memorial at the south end of Trônes Wood

At 7pm on 12 July part of the 7th Queen's were pinned down in front of Trônes Wood so they withdrew. The 7th Queen's secured the south-east corner of the wood while the 7th Buffs cleared part of Maltz Horn Trench.

> 18th (Eastern) Division, Major General Ivor Maxse
> 53 Brigade, 8th Norfolks, 8th Suffolks, 10th Essex, 6th Berkshires

54 Brigade, 11th Royal Fusiliers, 7th Bedfords, 8th Northants, 12th
Middlesex

55 Brigade, 7th Queen's, 7th Buffs, 8th East Surreys, 7th Queen's
Own

Pioneers, 8th Sussex: Artillery, LXXXII, LXXXIII, LXXXIV and
LXXXV Brigades

Memorial B: The 18th Division memorial is at the south-east corner of Trônes Wood. The division was engaged in the wood for three days, each time becoming disorientated in the smashed trees. The 12th Middlesex cleared it after Lieutenant Colonel Francis Maxwell VC (a Boer War award) announced 'I am going this night to instil the spirit of savagery into my battalion'.

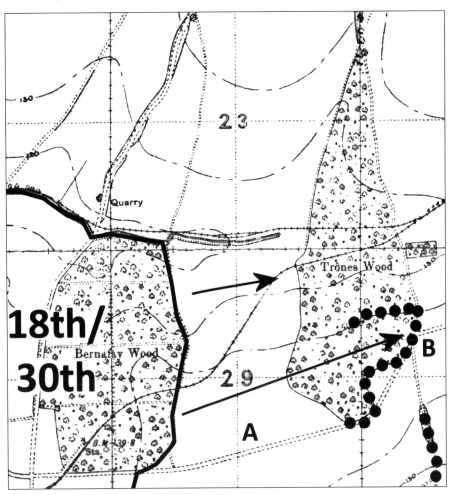

After occupying Bernafay Wood, XIII Corps struggled to clear Trônes Wood before 13 July.

3 to 11 July, X and III Corps

49th (West Riding) Division, Schwaben Redoubt
Viewpoint is off the map, see Viewpoint B on the 1 July X Corps' left flank map on page 23.

At 2.30am on 7 July the 1/4th KOYLI were driven back to the old front line despite reinforcements from the 1/5th KOYLIs and the 1/5th York and Lancasters.

> 49th Division, Major General Edward Perceval
> 146 Brigade, 1/5th, 1/6th, 1/7th and 1/8th West Yorkshires
> 147 Brigade, 1/4th, 1/5th, 1/6th and 1/7th Duke's
> 148 Brigade, 1/4th and 1/5th KOYLIs, 1/4th and 1/5th York and Lancasters
> Pioneers, 3rd Monmouths: Artillery, CCXLV, CCXLVI, CCXLVII, CCXLVIII Brigades

25th Division, Leipzig Salient
Viewpoint is off the map, see Viewpoint B on the 1 July X Corps' right flank map on page 24.

The 1st Wiltshires captured Hindenburg Trench late on 5 July.

> 25th Division, Major General Guy Bainbridge
> 7 Brigade, 10th Cheshires, 3rd Worcesters, 8th Loyals, 1st Wiltshires
> 74 Brigade, 11th Lancashire Fusiliers, 13th Cheshires, 9th Loyals, 2nd Irish Rifles
> 75 Brigade, 11th Cheshires, 8th Borders, 2nd South Lancashires, 8th South Lancashires
> Pioneers, 6th South Wales Borderers: Artillery, CX, CXI, CXII and CXIII Brigades

12th (Eastern) Division, Ovillers
Viewpoint A: Ovillers Military Cemetery
Viewpoint B: Lay-by, Ovillers road end
Viewpoint C: Gordon Dump Cemetery

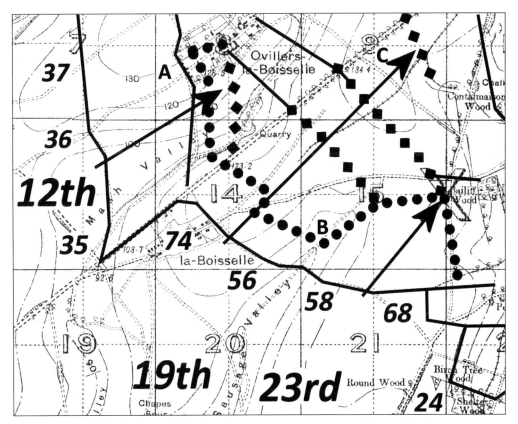

7 July X and III Corps: While 12th Division fought its way into Ovillers, 19th Division and 23rd Division edged towards Pozières.

At 3.15am on 3 July the 6th Queen's Own, 6th Queen's and 7th Suffolks captured two trenches. The 5th Berkshires reached Shrapnel Trench but the 6th Buffs were pinned down in no man's land and everyone fell back after a five-hour battle. The 9th Essex had advanced in the wrong direction across Mash Valley and they captured trenches north-east of La Boisselle.

The 9th Loyals, 13th Cheshires and 7th Suffolks advanced across Mash Valley at 8.05am on 7 July but they could not silence the machine guns north of La Boisselle. The 9th Royal Fusiliers and 7th Sussex captured three trenches west of Ovillers and were reinforced by the 11th Middlesex, 9th Essex and 7th Surrey; the 8th South Lancashires linked up the footholds.

At 3.45am on 8 July, the 7th East Surreys and the 9th Essex cleared the west end of Ovillers as the 8th South Lancashires, 2nd Irish Rifles and 13th

A machine gun team operates during a gas attack.

Cheshires advanced south-east of the village. At 8pm the 11th Lancashire Fusiliers advanced 600 metres north of Ovillers by mistake. They were reinforced by the 2nd Irish Rifles but few returned. The 13th Cheshires occupied the original objective.

12th (Eastern) Division, Major General Arthur Scott
35 Brigade, 7th Norfolks, 7th Suffolks, 9th Essex, 5th Berkshires
36 Brigade, 8th Royal Fusiliers, 9th Royal Fusiliers, 7th Sussex, 11th Middlesex
37 Brigade, 6th Queen's, 6th Buffs, 7th East Surreys, 6th Queen's Own
Pioneers, 5th Northants: Artillery, LXII, LXIII, LXIV and LXV Brigades

5 to 17 July, III Corps' Right

23rd Division, Contalmaison

Viewpoint A: Peake Wood Cemetery
Viewpoint B: Contalmaison Church

At 4am on 5 July the 9th Green Howards attacked Lincoln Redoubt and at 6.45am the 11th West Yorkshires and 10th Duke's bombers captured Horseshoe Trench only to lose it. The 9th Green Howards then captured Horseshoe Trench and Lincoln Redoubt. Second Lieutenant Donald Bell knocked out a machine gun post in the afternoon (he was killed a few days later and was posthumously awarded the Victoria Cross). Overnight the 12th Durhams occupied Triangle Trench.

At 9.15am on 7 July the 12th Durhams and the 11th Northumberland Fusiliers reached Bailiff Wood but abandoned it because it was under fire. Machine gun fire then stopped the 1st East Lancashires reaching Bailiff Wood. The 1st Worcesters entered Contalmaison but the 2nd Northants

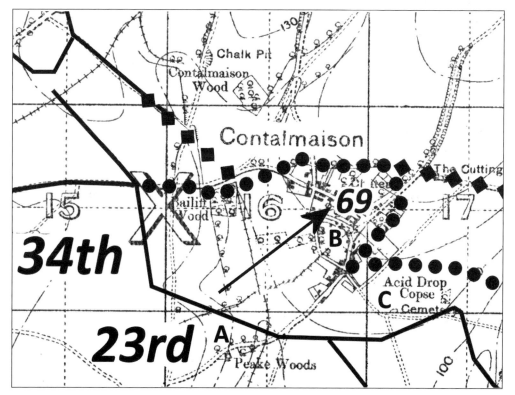

After several days fighting, 23rd Division captured Contalmaison on 11 July.

could not reach them, so the Worcesters withdrew when their ammunition ran out. They could not retake it later that evening.

A counter-attack from Contalmaison hit 68 Brigade on 10 July. At 4.30pm on 11 July machine gun fire stopped another counter-attack as the 11th West Yorkshires advanced from Bailiff Wood. The 9th Green Howards captured a trench north-west of Contalmaison but the 8th Green Howards were shot up cutting through a hedge woven with wire, to the south-west. The Germans then abandoned Contalmaison. At dusk the 12th Durhams surprised the Germans around Bailiff Wood while the 11th West Yorkshires and the 10th Duke's relieved the Green Howards in Contalmaison. Machine guns in Pozières Trench stopped the 12th Durhams advancing at 8pm on 17 July.

> 23rd Division, Major General James Babington
> 68 Brigade, 10th North'd Fusiliers, 11th North'd Fusiliers, 12th Durhams, 13th Durhams
> 69 Brigade, 11th West Yorkshires, 8th Green Howards, 9th Green Howards, 10th Duke's
> 70 Brigade, 11th Sherwoods, 8th KOYLIs, 8th York and Lancasters, 9th York and Lancasters
> Pioneers, 9th South Staffords: Artillery, CII, CIII, CIV and CV Brigades

Memorial C: The Bell's Redoubt memorial is on the Contalmaison to Fricourt road.

An 18-pounder field gun crew fires a protective barrage.

7 to 10 July, XV Corps' Left

17th (Northern) Division, Quadrangle Support Trench and Pearl Alley
Viewpoint A: Contalmaison civilian cemetery
Viewpoint B: Quadrangle Wood

The 10th Lancashire Fusiliers and 9th Northumberland Fusiliers charged Quadrangle Support at 2am on 7 July only to run into an attack by the Prussian Guard. There was a stalemate and reinforcements from the 10th Sherwoods failed to break it. The next attack was delayed to 8am but the troops heard about it late and half the 9th Duke's were unable to take part. The rest of the Duke's and the 12th Manchesters advanced a few minutes late and were shot down by machine guns in Mametz Wood. The 6th Dorsets were hit moving towards the west side of Mametz Wood and the 7th East Yorkshires could not clear Quadrangle Alley. The 10th Sherwood

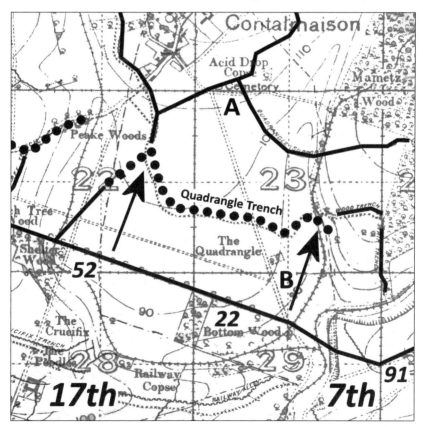

By 10 July, 17th Division had advanced up the slope to capture Quadrangle Trench and Quadrangle Support.

Foresters joined the Dorsets and East Yorkshires in a final attack at 8pm and captured part of Quadrangle Trench.

The following morning bombers could not clear Pearl Alley or Quadrangle Trench. The 6th Dorsets, 7th Green Howards and 7th East Yorkshires reached Quadrangle Support at 5.50pm; but the battered trench was knee deep in mud, so they withdrew. An hour later the Dorsets rushed Wood Trench and connected it to Quadrangle Trench.

At 11.20pm on 9 July the 8th South Staffords captured the west half of Quadrangle Support but the 7th Green Howards advanced late and were halted (the Green Howards believed the Staffords advanced early, alerting the Germans). The 7th East Yorkshires and 6th Dorsets failed to take the rest of the trench so the Staffords withdrew. Bombers eventually cleared Quadrangle Support on the afternoon of 10 July.

> 17th (Northern) Division, Major General Thomas Pilcher
> Major General Philip Robertson from 12 July
> 50 Brigade, 10th West Yorkshires, 7th East Yorkshires, 7th Green Howards, 6th Dorsets
> 51 Brigade, 7th Lincolns, 7th Borders, 8th South Staffords, 10th Sherwoods
> 52 Brigade, 9th North'd Fusiliers, 10th Lancashire Fusiliers, 9th Duke's, 12th Manchesters
> Pioneers, 7th York and Lancasters: Artillery, LXXVIII, LXXIX, LXXX and LXXXI Brigades

The 12th Manchesters have a memorial in Contalmaison civilian cemetery.

The Welsh Dragon memorial at Mametz Wood.

7 to 10 July, XV Corps' Right

38th (Welsh) Division, Mametz Wood
Viewpoint A: Welsh Division dragon memorial

Wind dispersed the smoke screen covering the 11th SWBs and 16th Welsh as they advanced towards the Hammerhead at 8.30am on 7 July and they were pinned down. The 10th SWBs supported further attacks at 10.15am and 3.15pm but they could not reach the Hammerhead. The 14th Welsh Fusiliers were supposed to clear the south half of the wood on the evening of 8 July but the order was based on reports that the Germans had abandoned the wood. They had not. Only a platoon was sent forward and it returned an hour later, reporting they were unable find a way into the wood. Major General Phillips was dismissed on 9 July and temporarily replaced by Major General Herbert Watts, 7th Division's commander.

Zero hour was set for 4.15am on 10 July but late orders meant the 16th Welsh Fusiliers were delayed. They were pinned down until the 14th Welsh Fusiliers carried them into the wood; the 15th Welsh Fusiliers then reinforced the advance. The 14th Welsh entered the east side of the wood but the 13th Welsh were pinned down in front of the Hammerhead until the 10th Welsh closed the gap between the brigades.

There was a two hour delay waiting for the barrage to lift and the Germans reoccupied Mametz Wood. The Welshmen found it impossible to clear it until the 17th Welsh Fusiliers and 10th SWBs reinforced the line. At 4.30pm the 17th Welsh Fusiliers and 14th Welsh advanced to the north edge of the wood, only to withdraw inside due to heavy fire. Meanwhile, the 10th SWBs cleared the Hammerhead.

At 3.30pm on 11 July, the 16th, 10th and 15th Welsh reached the north edge of the wood as the 11th SWBs advanced on the right. They again had to abandon the edge of the wood during the night. Major General Charles Blackader took over 38th Division after it withdrew.

> 38th (Welsh) Division, Major General Ivor Phillips (removed on 9 July)
> Major General Herbert Watts was the temporary commander
> 113 Brigade, 13th, 14th, 15th and 16th Welsh Fusiliers
> 114 Brigade, 10th, 13th, 14th and 15th Welsh
> 115 Brigade, 17th Welsh Fusiliers, 10th and 11th South Wales Borderers, 16th Welsh

Pioneers, 19th Welsh: Artillery, CXIX, CXX, CXXI and CXXII Brigades

Memorial A: The 38th (Welsh) Division's imposing dragon memorial is just south of the south-east corner of Mametz Wood.
Off Map: The 14th Royal Welsh Fusiliers memorial is in Dantzig Alley Cemetery, which overlooks Mametz Wood.

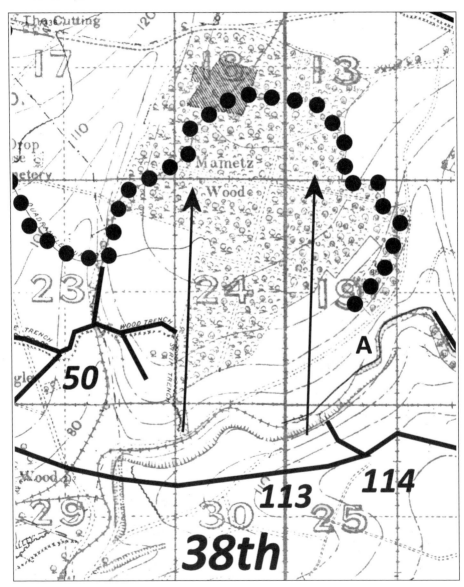

By 11 July, 38th (Welsh) Division had cleared Mametz Wood.

14 July, XV Corps

During the night infantry and engineering officers laid out white tapes so the men could deploy in silence 400 metres from the German line ready for zero hour at 3.25am.

21st Division, Bazentin le Petit
Viewpoint A: Hard-standing next to south edge of Bazentin-le-Petit Wood
Viewpoint B: Flat Iron Copse Cemetery
Viewpoint C: Bazentin-le-Petit Military Cemetery

The 7th Leicesters were pinned down north of Mametz Wood until their bombers cleared the German trench from the flanks. The 6th Leicesters advanced north of the Hammerhead into Bazentin-le-Petit Wood. The Leicesters then cleared the wood and Bazentin-le-Petit village.

> 21st Division, Major General David Campbell
> 62 Brigade, 12th and 13th Northumberland Fusiliers, 1st Lincolns, 10th Green Howards
> 64 Brigade, 9th and 10th KOYLIs, 14th and 15th Durhams
> 110 Brigade, 6th, 7th, 8th and 9th Leicesters
> Pioneers, 14th Northumberland Fusiliers: Artillery, XCIV, XCV, XCVI and XCVII Brigades

7th Division, Bazentin le Grand Wood
Viewpoint D: Bazentin-le-Petit Cemetery
Viewpoint E: Hard-standing on the crest north of Bazentin-le-Petit

The 8th Devons and 2nd Borders overran the Snout and Circus Trench and the Germans ran from Bazentin-le-Grand Wood. The 2nd Warwicks gave covering fire as the 2nd Irish Regiment cleared the east side of Bazentin-le-Petit Wood. It took until nightfall to clear the village with the 2nd Gordons.

Although High Wood was empty, the advance was postponed until Bazentin-le-Petit and Longueval were cleared.

The Germans had occupied the wood when the 1st South Staffords and 2nd Queen's advanced towards it at 6.15pm. The Queen's dug in on the west side while the Staffords fought in the trees, with the help of 22nd Manchesters. Although 33rd Division never received any orders to deploy,

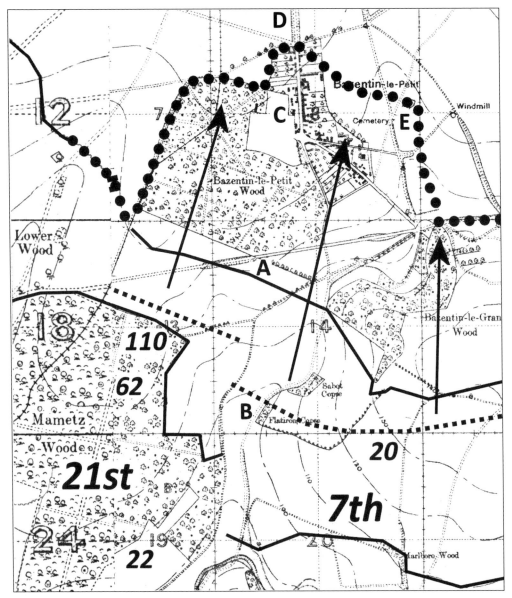

14 July, XV Corps: As 21st Division advanced through Bazentin le Petit Wood, 7th Division moved through Bazentin le Grand Wood.

the 1st Queen's and the 1/9th HLI filled the gap between Bazentin-le-Petit and High Wood after 7th Division requested help.

7th Division, Major General Herbert Watts

20 Brigade, 8th Devons, 9th Devons, 2nd Borders, 2nd Gordons

22 Brigade, 2nd Warwicks, 2nd Irish Regiment, 1st Welsh Fusiliers, 20th Manchesters

91 Brigade, 2nd Queen's, 1st South Staffords, 21st Manchesters, 22nd Manchesters

Pioneers, 24th Manchesters: Artillery, XIV (RHA), XXII and XXXV Brigades

2nd Indian Cavalry Division, High Wood

The 20th Deccan Horse and 7th Dragoon Guards came under fire from infantry hiding in the long grass when they advanced east of High Wood. The 7th Dragoon Guards dug in at nightfall, while the rest of the division returned to their bivouacs.

Indian cavalry practice a charge.

14 July, XIII Corps

During the night white tapes were laid down so that the men could deploy close to the German line, ready for zero hour at 3.25am.

3rd Division, Bazentin-le-Grand
Viewpoint A: Hard-standing south of Bazentin-le-Grand by a solitary tree
Viewpoint B: Crucifix Corner, Bazentin-le-Grand

The 12th West Yorkshires and 13th King's charged the enemy trench and the 1st Northumberland Fusiliers connected them. The West Yorkshires cleared Bazentin-le-Grand Wood and the King's cleared the village, followed by the Northumberland Fusiliers. The 7th Shropshires and 8th East Yorkshires were pinned down until the 1st Scots Fusiliers' bombers cleared the German trench.

> 3rd Division, Major General Aylmer Haldane
> 8 Brigade, 2nd Royal Scots, 8th East Yorkshires, 1st Scots
>   Fusiliers, 7th Shropshires
> 9 Brigade, 1st Northumberland Fusiliers, 4th Royal Fusiliers, 13th
>   King's, 12th West Yorkshires
> 76 Brigade, 8th King's Own, 2nd Suffolks, 10th Welsh Fusiliers,
>   1st Gordons
> Pioneers, 20th KRRC: Artillery, XXIII, XL and XLI Brigades

9th (Scottish) Division, Longueval
Viewpoint C: Caterpillar Valley Cemetery
Viewpoint D: Longueval Road Cemetery

The 9th Scottish Rifles and 11th Royal Scots cleared the trenches west of Longueval. The 10th Argylls advanced to Clarges Street as the 8th Black Watch and 7th Seaforths cleared the south half of Longueval. The 12th Royal Scots could not cross the square but the 1st South Africans fought through the night to clear the village. The Seaforths and 5th Camerons could not reach Waterlot Farm, south-east of the village, but they took Longueval Alley.

> 9th (Scottish) Division, Major General William Furse
> 26 Brigade, 8th Black Watch, 7th Seaforths, 5th Camerons, 10th
>   Argylls

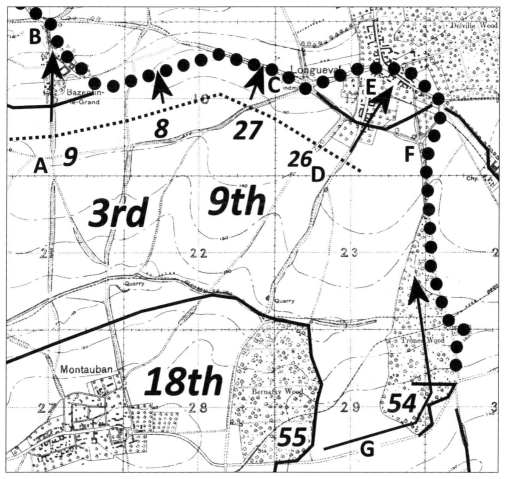

14 July, XIII Corps: 18th Division cleared Trônes Wood just in time but while 3rd Division cleared its objectives early, 9th Division had a prolonged battle for Longueval.

27 Brigade, 11th and 12th Royal Scots, 6th KOSBs, 9th Scottish Rifles
South African Brigade, 1st, 2nd, 3rd and 4th South African
Pioneers, 9th Seaforths: Artillery, L, LI, LII and LIII Brigades

Memorial E: A memorial to all pipers stands in Longueval square

18th (Eastern) Division, Trônes Wood
Viewpoint F: Rue de Clos, the Trônes Wood road out of Longueval
Viewpoint G: Between bottom corners of Bernafay Wood and Trônes Wood, north view

The 6th Northants and 12th Middlesex started entering Trônes Wood at 3.40am on 14 July only to reach the south-east corner rather than the north end. Lieutenant Colonel Francis Maxwell VC (awarded in the Boer War) and the Middlesex had cleared the wood by 9.30am. A wounded Sergeant William Boulter silenced a machine gun team en route and was awarded the Victoria Cross.

18th (Eastern) Division, Major General Ivor Maxse
53 Brigade, 8th Norfolks, 8th Suffolks, 10th Essex, 6th Berkshires
54 Brigade, 11th Royal Fusiliers, 7th Bedfords, 8th Northants,
    12th Middlesex
55 Brigade, 7th Queen's, 7th Buffs, 8th East Surreys, 7th Queen's
    Own
Pioneers, 8th Sussex: Artillery, LXXXII, LXXXIII, LXXXIV and
    LXXXV Brigades

A 60-pounder gun silhouetted against the horizon.

15 July, III Corps

34th Division, Contalmaison
Viewpoint A: Pozières British Cemetery
Viewpoint B: Sunken Road Cemeteries

At 9.20am the 8th East Lancashires advanced from between Contalmaison and Bailiff Wood but they were unable to reach Pozières Trench. The 10th Royal Fusiliers tried at 6pm but their damp flares would not light, so platoons advanced at different times and were brought to a halt one by one. A new trench facing Pozières Trench was dug overnight.

> 34th Division, Major General Edward Ingouville-Williams
> 101 Brigade, 15th and 16th Royal Scots, 10th Lincolns, 11th Suffolks
> 102 (Tyneside Scottish) Brigade, 20th, 21st, 22nd and 23rd Northumberland Fusiliers
> 103 (Tyneside Irish) Brigade, 24th, 25th, 26th and 27th Northumberland Fusiliers
> Pioneers, 18th Northumberland Fusiliers: Artillery, CLII, CLX, CLXXV and CLXXVI Brigades

Memorial A: Pozières British Cemetery stands next to the Albert road, south-west of Pozières. The surrounding Memorial to the Missing remembers 14,691 men with no known graves who lost their lives in the spring battles of 1918, when the Germans overran the 1916 Somme battlefield. Most of the 2,758 graves were moved here after the Armistice and nearly half are unidentified.

There are a lot of Australian graves in the cemetery, mostly dating from the July and August battle, but the names of the missing are carved on the Australian National Memorial at Villers-Bretonneux, twenty miles to the south-west, the site of Australian battles in April and August 1918.

Memorial C: There are two memorials next to Contalmaison church remembering the 16th Royal Scots, which was known as McCrae's Battalion. Members were footballers and supporters from the Edinburgh area. The 15th Royal Scots, City of Edinburgh Battalion, is also remembered.

1st Division, Bazentin-le-Petit Wood and Munster Alley
Viewpoint D: Hard-standing on the site of Contalmaison Chateau

At 9am on 15 July the 1st Loyals were clearing the OG1 and OG2 lines until the British barrage forced them to withdraw. The 2nd Welsh could not get any further during the afternoon. The following morning the Welsh could not take the German Second Line west of Bazentin-le-Petit Wood because the trench had become a muddy ditch.

At 11.50pm on 16 July the 2nd Munsters and the 1st Gloucesters overran the German Second Line but a request to push into Pozières was denied. The 1st SWBs also occupied Black Watch Alley on the left. The Munsters tried in vain to capture the junction of Munster Alley and OG2.

1st Division, Major General Peter Strickland
1 Brigade, 10th Gloucesters, 1st Black Watch, 8th Berkshires, 1st
    Camerons
2 Brigade, 2nd Sussex, 1st Loyals, 1st Northants, 2nd KRRC
3 Brigade, 1st South Wales Borderers, 1st Gloucesters, 2nd Welsh,
    2nd Munsters
Pioneers, 1/6th Welsh: Artillery, XXV, XXVI and XXXIX Brigades

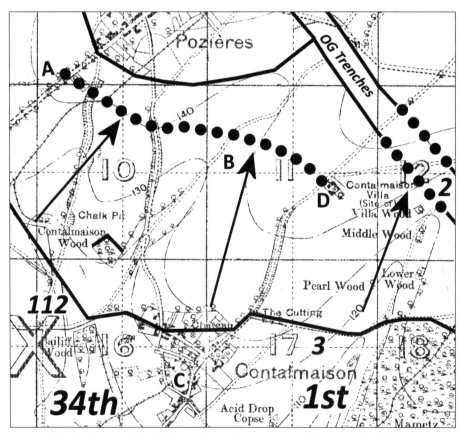

15 July, III Corps: 34th Division made good progress towards Pozières but 1st Division faced a long struggle to clear the OG Trenches.

15 July, XV Corps

33rd Division, the Switch Line
Viewpoint A: Hard-standing on the road north of Bazentin-le-Petit

At 9am the 1st Middlesex were pinned down north of Bazentin-le-Petit and the 1st Queen's were stopped by wire in the long grass. The 1/9th Highland Light Infantry were unable to clear the west edge of High Wood. All three battalions were pinned down in front of the Switch Line and the 2nd Worcesters and 16th KRRC were pinned down when they tried to reinforce the line. The survivors withdrew during the night.

33rd Division, Major General Herman Landon
98 Brigade, 4th King's, 1/4th Suffolks, 1st Middlesex, 2nd Argylls
100 Brigade, 1st Queen's, 2nd Worcesters, 16th KRRC, 1/9th HLI
19 Brigade, 20th Royal Fusiliers, 2nd Welsh Fusiliers, 1st and 1/5th Scottish Rifles
Pioneers, 18th Middlesex: Artillery, CLVI, CLXII, CLXVI and CLXVII Brigades

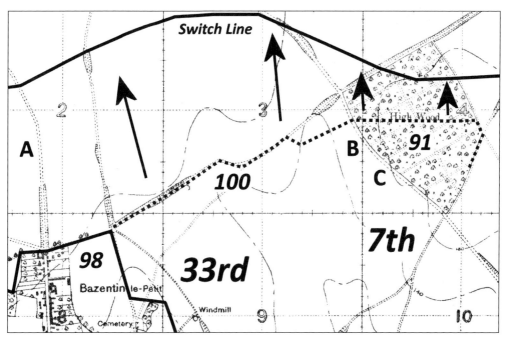

15 July, XV Corps: The opportunity of a breakthrough had passed by the time 33rd Division advanced towards the Switch Line and 7th Division moved into High Wood.

Waiting for the next push in a makeshift trench.

Memorial B: The 1/9th HLI Glasgow Highlanders cairn is on the south-west edge of High Wood

7th Division, High Wood
Viewpoint C: London Cemetery and Extension, south-west side of High Wood

The 1st South Staffords and 2nd Queen's advance through High Wood failed to reach the Switch Line and the 21st Manchesters had to reinforce the line. A German counter-attack drove them back, so the 22nd Manchesters were sent forward. A second attempt to retake the Switch Line at 4.45pm also failed. The troops then withdrew from the wood so that the artillery could shell it all night.

> 7th Division, Major General Herbert Watts
> 20 Brigade, 8th and 9th Devons, 2nd Borders, 2nd Gordons
> 22 Brigade, 2nd Warwicks, 2nd Irish Regiment, 1st Welsh
>   Fusiliers, 20th Manchesters
> 91 Brigade, 2nd Queen's, 1st South Staffords, 21st and 22nd
>   Manchesters
> Pioneers, 24th Manchesters: Artillery, XIV, XXII and XXXV
>   Brigades

15 to 18 July, XIII Corps

9th (Scottish) Division, Longueval and Delville Wood
Viewpoint A: Longueval square
Viewpoint B: South African Memorial, Delville Wood

Barbed wire woven into the hedges stopped the 12th Royal Scots, while the square in Longueval was a killing zone. At 6.15am the 2nd, 3rd and part of the 4th South African Regiments advanced along the chateau drive and cleared most of Delville Wood. The 1st South African Regiment reinforced them when the Germans counter-attacked. Parts of the 5th Camerons and 4th South African Regiment failed to capture Waterlot Farm (Sugar Refinery).

At 10am on 16 July the 11th Royal Scots could not clear the orchards west of Longueval while the 1st South African Regiment could not clear the rest of Delville Wood. At 2am on 17 July the 12th Royal Scots and the 6th KOSBs advanced astride North Street. But they missed many dugouts in the rain and the Germans emerged as flares lit up the sky. South African attacks from the Strand and Prince's Street also failed. At 9am on 17 July the 7th Seaforths and 4th South African Regiment secured Waterlot Farm.

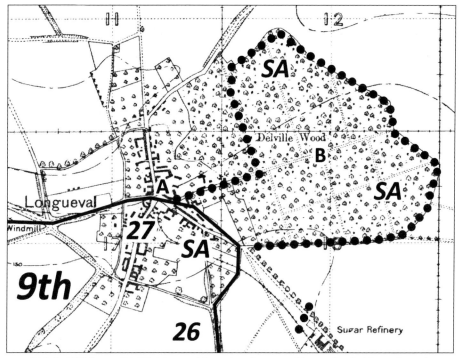

15 July, XIII Corps: 9th Division could not clear Longueval but its South African Brigade captured most of Delville Wood.

At 3.30pm on 18 July the Germans captured most of Longueval and drove the South Africans back to Prince's Street. Private William Faulds rescued many injured of the 1st South African Regiment; he was awarded the Victoria Cross. At 6pm the 8th Black Watch, 7th Seaforths and 5th Camerons cleared Longueval. Machine gun fire delayed the 8th Norfolks and they missed the barrage. Their left was stopped at the chateau but the right advanced through the south side of the wood, followed by the 10th Essex and the 6th Berkshires.

9th (Scottish) Division, Major General William Furse
26 Brigade, 8th Black Watch, 7th Seaforths, 5th Camerons, 10th
    Argylls
27 Brigade, 11th and 12th Royal Scots, 6th KOSBs, 9th Scottish
    Rifles
South African Brigade, 1st, 2nd, 3rd and 4th South African
Pioneers, 9th Seaforths: Artillery, L, LI, LII and LIII Brigades
    Attached from 18th (Eastern) Division
53 Brigade, 8th Norfolks, 8th Suffolks, 10th Essex, 6th Berkshires

Memorial B: It took six weeks to clear Delville Wood, or Devil's Wood, but it will forever be connected with the South African Brigade. Only 750 of over 3,150 South Africans who had been committed answered the roll call after six days' fighting. The South African Armed Forces Museum is a replica of the star-shaped Castle of Good Hope at Cape Town and it houses displays commemorating the South African forces deeds in both world wars.

The South African memorial in Delville Wood.

20 July, XV Corps

33rd Division, High Wood
Viewpoint A: 47th (2nd London) Division memorial, south west edge of High Wood

At dusk the 2nd Worcesters established a line between Bazentin-le-Petit and High Wood. The troops detailed to clear the wood received their orders late and they had to march over three miles through the mist to reach High Wood. The Scots crawled the final 100 metres while the British artillery shelled High Wood and charged through the trees when the guns lifted at 3.25am. The 5/6th and 1st Scottish Rifles fought for the Switch Line as the 20th Royal Fusiliers occupied the south half of the wood.

A counter-attack around 8am overran the 5/6th Scottish Rifles so the 2nd Welsh Fusiliers entered the wood at midday, joining the 'hopeless mix up of bush fighting'. The Welsh Fusiliers captured the Switch Line and dug new trenches but lost them before the 16th KRRC and 1st Queen's reached High Wood at dusk. Captain Robert Graves of the Welsh Fusiliers was badly injured during the fighting. He was reported as having died of wounds, but he survived to write many poems and books.

> 33rd Division, Major General Herman Landon
> 98 Brigade, 4th King's, 1/4th Suffolks, 1st Middlesex, 2nd Argylls
> 100 Brigade, 1st Queen's, 2nd Worcesters, 16th KRRC, 1/9th HLI
> 19 Brigade, 20th Royal Fusiliers, 2nd Welsh Fusiliers, 1st Scottish Rifles, 1/5th Scottish Rifles
> Pioneers, 18th Middlesex: Artillery, CLVI, CLXII, CLXVI and CLXVII Brigades

7th Division, Wood Lane
Viewpoint B: Caterpillar Valley Cemetery

The 2nd Gordons and the 8th Devons crawled through the mist for twenty minutes before rushing the trench along Black Road at 3.25am. They then came under fire from the strongpoint at the east corner of High Wood and machine gun teams in the grass in front of Wood Lane. Private Theodore Veale went to look for his injured officer but could not rescue him, so he returned with help. He used his Lewis gun to keep the Germans at bay while his comrades rescued Lieutenant Savill. Veale was awarded the Victoria Cross.

7th Division, Major General Herbert Watts

20 Brigade, 8th Devons, 9th Devons, 2nd Borders, 2nd Gordons

22 Brigade, 2nd Warwicks, 2nd Irish Regiment, 1st Welsh Fusiliers, 20th Manchesters

91 Brigade, 2nd Queen's, 1st South Staffords, 21st Manchesters, 22nd Manchesters

Pioneers, 24th Manchesters: Artillery, XIV, XXII and XXXV Brigades

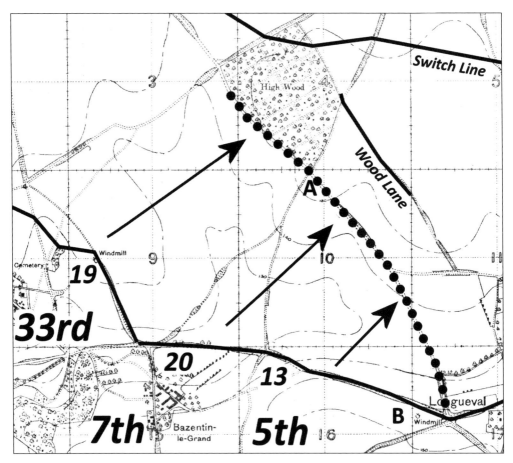

20 July, XV Corps: While 33rd Division could not secure a foothold in High Wood, neither 7th Division nor 5th Division could reach Wood Lane.

18 to 20 July, XIII Corps

3rd Division, Longueval and Delville Wood
Viewpoint A: Crucifix north of Longueval
Viewpoint B: The square in Longueval
Viewpoint C: South African Memorial, Delville Wood

At 3.45am on 18 July the 1st Gordons and 8th King's Own bypassed the wired hedges, cleared North Street and dug in along Duke Street. The 2nd Suffolks attacked the west side of Longueval through the mist at 3.35am on 20 July but few returned. The 10th Welsh Fusiliers' guide lost his way and flares lit up the sky when they charged across the village square and along the chateau driveway ten minutes late. The 11th Essex did not know about the Welsh attack and many were hit by 'friendly fire' before the shooting stopped.

Most of the Welsh fell back but some stayed all day in Delville Wood, including Corporal Joseph Davies and eight men. They kept the Germans at bay until Davies chased them away; he was awarded the Victoria Cross. Private Albert Hill drove off twenty Germans before fighting his way back to his company with his sergeant. He then rescued a mortally wounded Captain Scales before taking two prisoners; he was awarded the Victoria Cross.

Major Billy Congreve had helped to guide battalions into line and attended the wounded during the fighting around Longueval. He was killed on 20 July while gathering information on the failed attack; he was awarded the Victoria Cross.

3rd Division, Major General Aylmer Haldane
8 Brigade, 2nd Royal Scots, 8th East Yorkshires, 1st Scots Fusiliers, 7th Shropshires
9 Brigade, 1st Northumberland Fusiliers, 4th Royal Fusiliers, 13th King's, 12th West Yorkshires
76 Brigade, 8th King's Own, 2nd Suffolks, 10th Welsh Fusiliers, 1st Gordons
Pioneers, 20th KRRC: Artillery, XXIII, XL, and XLI Brigades

35th Division, Guillemont
Viewpoint D: Guillemont Road Cemetery
Viewpoint E: Pull in before the Crucifix next to Lonely Trench

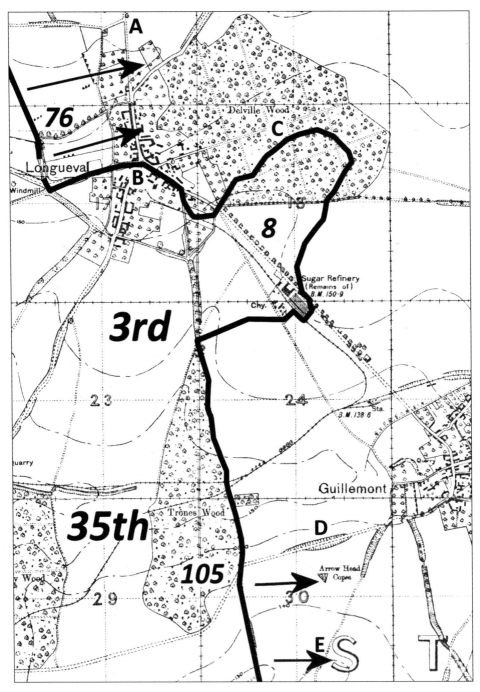

20 July, XIII Corps: 35th Division's scaled down attack failed to gain any ground south of Guillemont.

Zero hour was 5am and the batteries fired blindly into the thick mist for thirty minutes. Gas shells incapacitated half the 15th Sherwoods and the sun had risen by the time the rest advanced from Trônes Wood. They could not capture the trenches south of Arrow Head Copse or Maltz Horn Farm. Two 23rd Manchester companies made another attempt at 11.35am, only to find the trench south of Arrow Head Copse had been obliterated.

35th Division, Major General Reginald Pinney
104 Brigade, 17th, 18th and 20th Lancashire Fusiliers, 23rd Manchesters
105 Brigade, 15th and 16th Cheshires, 14th Gloucesters, 15th Sherwoods
106 Brigade, 17th Royal Scots, 17th West Yorkshires, 19th Durhams, 18th HLI
Pioneers, 19th North'd Fusiliers: Artillery, CLVII, CLVIII, CLVIX and CLXIII Brigades

Relaying signals to the rear.

9 to 22 July, X Corps

32nd, 25th and 48th Divisions, Ovillers

Viewpoint A: Ovillers Military Cemetery
Viewpoint B: Authuille road north of Ovillers, turn to the right, pull in on the left after 200 metres
Viewpoint C: Lay-by opposite Ovillers road junction with the Bapaume road.

The three divisions of the Corps contributed battalions to the battle for Ovillers. The 2nd Manchesters, 1st Dorsets and 15th HLI made little headway on 9 and 10 July. The 11th Cheshires and 8th Loyals also failed on 10 July and the 3rd Worcesters had to hold the line. Late on 10/11 July the 2nd Inniskillings advanced north-west of Ovillers and two nights later the 8th Borders captured the trench west of the village, so that the 2nd South Lancashires could enter the ruins.

On 14 July the 3rd Worcesters captured a trench north-east of Ovillers as the 1st Dorsets cleared trenches west of the village. The 1/7th Warwicks and 10th Cheshires advanced to the south-east and the 8th Borders gained ground to the south. At 2am on 15 July, 32nd Division attacked south-west of Ovillers and 25th Division tried to advance on the east side; neither went far.

The 48th Division carried out a surprise attack against Ovillers at 1am on 16 July. The 1/5th Warwicks advanced to the north-east, the 1/4th Gloucesters to the west and the 1/7th Worcesters to the south. The garrison surrendered to the 11th Lancashire Fusiliers' bombers after two weeks of fighting.

On 20 July the 1/4th Gloucesters cleared trenches north of Ovillers and the 1/5th and 1/6th Gloucesters advanced north of the village the following day. The barrage started two minutes early at 2.43am on 22 July, alerting the Germans, and they halted the Gloucesters and Worcesters; they withdrew three hours later.

32nd Division, Major General William Rycroft
14 Brigade, 19th Lancashire Fusiliers, 1st Dorsets, 2nd Manchesters, 15th HLI
96 Brigade, 16th North'd Fusiliers, 15th and 16th Lancashire Fusiliers, 2nd Inniskillings
97 Brigade, 11th Borders, 2nd KOYLIs, 16th and 17th HLI
Pioneers, 17th Northumberland Fusiliers: Artillery, CLV, CLXI, CLXIV, CLXVIII Brigades

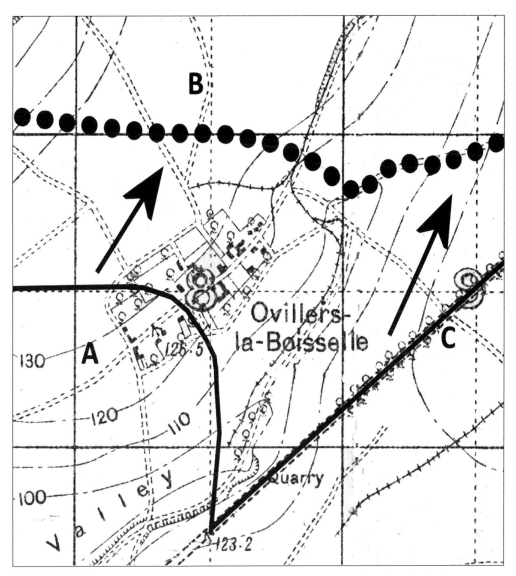

9 and 22 July, X Corps: 32nd, 25th and 48th Divisions struggled to clear the Ovillers area.

25th Division, Major General Guy Bainbridge
7 Brigade, 10th Cheshires, 3rd Worcesters, 8th Loyals, 1st Wiltshires
74 Brigade, 11th Lancashire Fusiliers, 13th Cheshires, 9th Loyals, 2nd Irish Rifles

1st Australian Division's memorial at Pozières.

75 Brigade, 11th Cheshires, 8th Borders, 2nd South Lancashires,
   8th South Lancashires
Pioneers, 6th SWBs: Artillery, CX, CXI, CXII and CXIII Brigades

48th (South Midland) Division, Major General Robert Fanshawe
143 Brigade, 1/5th, 1/6th, 1/7th and 1/8th Warwicks
144 Brigade, 1/4th and 1/6th Gloucesters, 1/7th and 1/8th
   Worcesters
145 Brigade, 1/5th Gloucesters, 1/1st and 1/4th Ox & Bucks, 1/4th
   Berkshires
Pioneers, 1/5th Sussex: Artillery, CCXL, CCXLI, CCXLII and
   CCXLIII Brigades

23 and 25 July, I ANZAC Corps

1st Australian Division, Pozières
Viewpoint A: 1st Australian Division memorial, west end of Pozières
Viewpoint B: Sunken Road Cemetery, on a road south of the village
Viewpoint C: Pozières civilian cemetery, north of the village
Viewpoint D: Pozières windmill, east end of village

The Australians advanced towards Pozières, with the 2nd and 1st Australian Battalions on the left and the 11th and 9th Australian Battalions on the right. They overran Pozières trench and moved into the village. The 4th, 3rd, 12th and 10th Australian Battalions moved through to the Bapaume road at 1am and the Germans withdrew when their dawn counter-attack through the north-west side of Pozières failed. The advance resumed around 5pm and 2nd Australian Battalion occupied Cement House (Gibraltar), an observation point at the south-west corner of the village. The 8th Australian Battalion moved along the Mouquet Farm road as the 12th Australian Battalion cleared the north side of the Bapaume road.

The 9th Australian Battalion reached the junction of the OG trenches and Pozières Trench by dawn with 10th Battalion's help. Second Lieutenant Arthur Blackburn was awarded the Victoria Cross for securing the division's right flank. Private John Leak was awarded the Victoria Cross for containing the counter-attacks, but the Australians could not retake the OG trenches.

At 2am on 24 July the 5th, 10th and 9th Australian Battalions attacked the OG trenches. The 5th Australian Battalion's left got lost but the right captured OG1. OG2 had been obliterated, so the Australians fell back and were then bombed out of OG1. The 10th and 9th Australian Battalions connected the OG lines but they could not capture the junction of OG2 and Munster Alley.

A mix-up in orders delayed 4th Australian Battalion but 8th Australian Battalion advanced astride the Mouquet Farm road at 3.45am. Private Thomas Cooke fought alone with his Lewis gun near the village cemetery until he was killed; he was posthumously awarded the Victoria Cross.

The 11th Australian Battalion withdrew when it came under heavy artillery fire at dawn. Machine guns in OG1 stopped 12th Australian Battalion advancing north of the Bapaume road but the 6th Australian Battalion reinforced it and the 3rd Australian Battalion linked the two captured areas together.

1st Australian Division, Major General Harold Walker
1 (New South Wales) Brigade, 1st, 2nd, 3rd and 4th Battalions
2 (Victoria) Brigade, 5th, 6th, 7th and 8th Battalions
3 Brigade, 9th, 10th, 11th and 12th Battalions
Pioneers, 1st Australian Pioneer Battalion: Artillery, 1st, 2nd and
3rd Australian Brigades

Memorial A: The 1st Australian Division Memorial stands next to the ruins of the Gibraltar blockhouse. The King's Royal Rifle Corps memorial is across the Bapaume road.

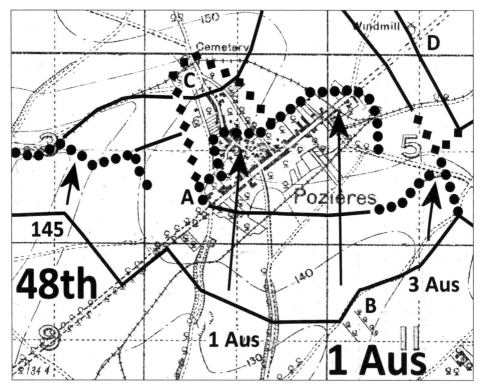

23 to 25 July, I ANZAC Corps: While 48th Division advanced west of Pozières, the 1st Australian Division cleared the village.

29 July to 4 August, I ANZAC Corps

2nd Australian Division, North and East of Pozières
Viewpoint A: Pozières civilian cemetery, north of the village
Viewpoint B: Pozières windmill, east of the village

The 23rd, 26th, 25th and 28th Australian Battalions crept towards the OG trenches at midnight on 29 July but they were spotted and flares lit up no man's land. The barrage intensified at 12.14am and one minute later the Australians overran the German outposts. The 23rd Battalion missed their objective and two waves kept going, never to be seen again. OG1 trench was cleared but wire stopped 26th, 25th and 28th Battalions reaching OG2 trench and they fell back to their own trenches, leaving 23rd Battalion in a salient north of the cemetery.

No man's land was too narrow for artillery support south of the Bapaume road and the trench mortars failed to suppress the Germans; neither 20th nor 17th Australian Battalions reached the OG1 trenches. Sergeant Claud Castleton was carrying his third wounded man on his back when he was killed; he was posthumously awarded the Victoria Cross.

At 9.15pm on 4 August wind dispersed the smoke on the left and machine gun fire prevented 23rd Australian Battalion blocking the OG Trenches along the Courcelette track. The 22nd, 26th, 25th and 27th Australian Battalions captured the OG1 and OG2 trenches north-east of Pozières. 27th Battalion had to dig a new trench around Pozières Mill because the German ones had been obliterated.

The 18th and 20th Australian Battalions overran OG1 south of the Bapaume road but some men advanced into their protective barrage, having failed to notice an obliterated OG2, and withdrew. Counter-attacks around dawn were repelled.

2nd Australian Division, Major General James Legge
5 (New South Wales) Brigade, 17th, 18th, 19th and 20th Australian
    Battalions
6 (Victoria) Brigade, 21st, 22nd, 23rd and 24th Australian
    Battalions
7 Brigade, 25th, 26th, 27th and 28th Australian Battalions
Pioneers, 2nd Australian Pioneer Battalion: Artillery, 4th, 5th and
    6th Australian Brigades

Memorial B: The Pozières Australian Memorial stands just north of the Bapaume road, on the east side of Pozières. It is on the site of Pozières Mill. The mill stood on the OG (Original German) Trench system, which was captured by the 2nd Australian Division on 4 August 1916. The Australians captured 1,500 metres of trenches in less than an hour, taking over 500 prisoners. They could see Courcelette but the German artillery could shell the captured trenches, making them a death trap.

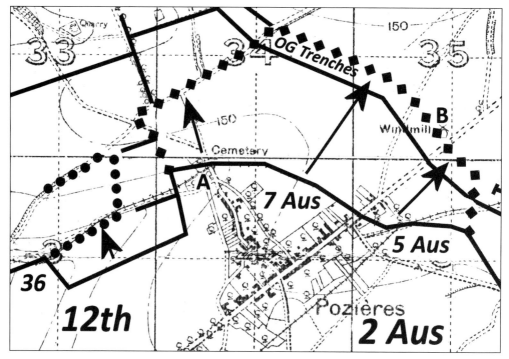

29 July, I ANZAC Corps: While 12th Division made progress west of Pozières, 2nd Australian Division captured the OG Trenches, at their second attempt, on 4 August.

23 to 26 July, III Corps

1st Division, Munster Alley and the Switch Line

Viewpoint A: Pull-in on the Pozières–Bazentin road, west of the Martinpuich road intersection

The troops were spotted assembling and lit up by flares when they advanced at 12.30am on 23 July. The 2nd Sussex and the 2nd KRRC were pinned down between Munster Alley and the Switch Line. The 10th Gloucesters and 1st Camerons were halted by machine guns hidden in the grass in front of the Switch Line.

Machine guns around Pozières windmill prevented the 1st SWBs reaching Munster Alley at 2am on 25 July. The 2nd Welsh advanced without a barrage at 3am the following morning and took the Germans by surprise, allowing them to contact the Australians on their left. The 23rd Division took over on 26 July but the 2nd Welsh remained behind to capture more ground with Australian help. The fighting lasted well into the night.

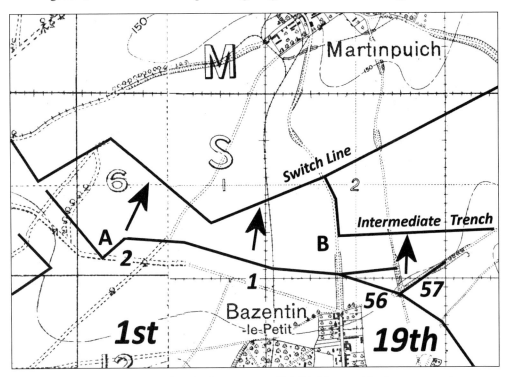

23 July, III Corps: Neither 1st Division nor 19th Division could advance towards Martinpuich.

1st Division, Major General Peter Strickland

1 Brigade, 10th Gloucesters, 1st Black Watch, 8th Berkshires, 1st Camerons

2 Brigade, 2nd Sussex, 1st Loyals, 1st Northants, 2nd KRRC

3 Brigade, 1st South Wales Borderers, 1st Gloucesters, 2nd Welsh, 2nd Munsters

Pioneers, 1/6th Welsh: Artillery, XXV, XXVI, XXXIX and LXI Brigades

19th (Western) Division, Intermediate Trench

Viewpoint B: The road north from Bazentin-le-Petit to the hard-standing on the crest

The 7th South Lancashires and 7th Loyals were unable to reach Intermediate Trench. The 8th Gloucesters and 10th Warwicks were supposed to crawl as close to the Switch Line as possible before zero hour. But the Warwicks had not relieved the 10th Worcesters in time and the Gloucesters were hit by crossfire from Intermediate Trench and High Wood.

19th (Western) Division, Major General Tom Bridges

56 Brigade, 7th King's Own, 7th East Lancashires, 7th South Lancashires, 7th Loyals

57 Brigade, 10th Warwicks, 8th Gloucesters, 10th Worcesters, 8th North Staffords

58 Brigade, 9th Cheshires, 9th Welsh Fusiliers, 9th Welsh, 6th Wiltshires

Pioneers, 5th SWBs: Artillery, LXXXVI, LXXXVII, LXXXVIII and LXXXIX Brigades

Highlanders making the best of what little they have.

30 July, III Corps

23rd Division, Munster Alley
Viewpoint A: Pull-in on the Pozières–Bazentin road, west of the Martinpuich road intersection

During the night of 28/29 July the 10th Duke's bombed along Munster Trench and advanced over the top, nearly reaching the Switch Line.

23rd Division, Major General James Babington
68 Brigade, 10th and 11th Northumberland Fusiliers, 12th and 13th Durhams
69 Brigade, 11th West Yorkshires, 8th Green Howards, 9th Green Howards, 10th Duke's
70 Brigade, 11th Sherwoods, 8th KOYLIs, 8th York and Lancasters, 9th York and Lancasters
Pioneers, 9th South Staffords: Artillery, CII, CIII, CIV and CV Brigades

19th (Western) Division, Intermediate Trench
Viewpoint B: Hard-standing on the track north of Bazentin-le-Petit

At 4.45am on 30 July the 10th Worcesters and 8th Gloucesters missed the barrage in the mist and were pinned down in front of Intermediate Trench. The 7th King's Own and 10th Warwicks advanced on time and captured their half of Intermediate Trench. The 5th SWBs helped them hold it. Private James Miller was hit in the abdomen as he carried a message back to the King's Own headquarters. He delivered the note but then collapsed and died. Private Miller was awarded the Victoria Cross.

19th (Western) Division, Major General Tom Bridges
56 Brigade, 7th King's Own, 7th East Lancashires, 7th South Lancashires, 7th Loyals
57 Brigade, 10th Warwicks, 8th Gloucesters, 10th Worcesters, 8th North Staffords
58 Brigade, 9th Cheshires, 9th Welsh Fusiliers, 9th Welsh, 6th Wiltshires
Pioneers, 5th SWBs: Artillery, LXXXVI, LXXXVII, LXXXVIII and LXXXIX Brigades

34th Division, Intermediate Trench
Viewpoint C: Hook Trench, west of High Wood

The 16th Royal Scots failed to bomb along Intermediate Trench on the nights of 1/2 and 2/3 August. The 11th Suffolks were supposed to attack at 2.30am on 4 August but only one company did and it had to withdraw. The three remaining companies attacked in daylight and they suffered dearly. Later that evening the 15th Royal Scots' bombers cleared another fifty metres of Intermediate Trench. The 8th East Lancashires' bombers failed to make progress on the morning of 7 August but the 10th Loyals captured another 200 metres during the early hours of the 11 August. Two nights later the 11th Warwicks failed to take any more ground.

> 34th Division, Major General Cecil Nicholson (Major General Ingouville-Williams was killed on 22 July)
> 101 Brigade, 15th and 16th Royal Scots, 10th Lincolns, 11th Suffolks
> 102 (Tyneside Scottish) Brigade, 20th, 21st, 22nd and 23rd Northumberland Fusiliers
> 103 (Tyneside Irish) Brigade, 24th, 25th, 26th and 27th Northumberland Fusiliers
> Pioneers, 18th North'd Fusiliers: Artillery, CLII, CLX, CLXXV and CLXXVI Brigades

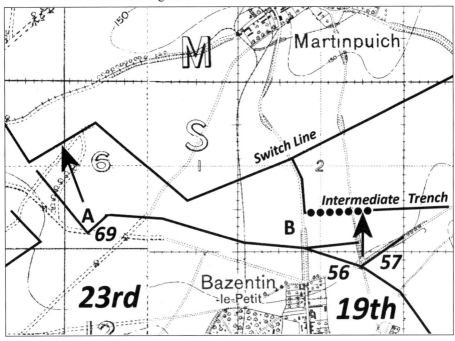

30 July, III Corps: Again, little progress was made towards Martinpuich.

23 July, XV Corps' Left

51st (Highland) Division, High Wood
Viewpoint A: 47th (2nd London) Division memorial, near south corner of High Wood

Flares lit up the advance at 12.45am on 27 July. Machine guns at the east end of Intermediate Trench cut up the 1/9th Royal Scots while the 1/4th Gordons were halted in front of the Switch Line.

At 9.20pm on 29 July a party of the 1/4th Seaforths failed to capture the strongpoint at the east corner of High Wood. Artillery fire forced the trench mortar teams to withdraw the following morning and the 1/7th Black Watch also failed to take it at 6.10am. The 1/6th Black Watch and 1/5th Gordons were pinned down in front of the wire covering Wood Lane.

> 51st (Highland) Division, Major General George Harper
> 152 Brigade, 1/5th and 1/6th Seaforths, 1/8th Argylls and 1/6th Gordons
> 153 Brigade, 1/6th and 1/7th Black Watch, 1/5th and 1/7th Gordons
> 154 Brigade, 1/4th Seaforths, 1/4th Gordons, 1/9th Royal Scots, 1/7th Argylls
> Pioneers, 1/8th Royal Scots: Artillery, CCLV, CCLVI, CCLVIII and CCLX Brigades

Memorial B: The High Wood Craters are at the east corner of the wood. The wood is private land but you can see the two water-filled craters just inside the trees. It is worth walking along the track on the east side of High Wood to get a better appreciation of the area north and east of the wood. From the east corner you can see the German side of the slope which the British artillery struggled to target. Delville Wood is to the south-east and Flers is to the north-east.

5th Division's Left, Wood Lane
Viewpoint A: London memorial, south corner of High Wood
Viewpoint C: Crucifix north of Longueval

The 1st Queen's Own and 14th Warwicks advanced at 10pm on 23 July but flares meant they were hit by machine guns in High Wood and Wood Lane. The Queen's Own reached Wood Lane but had to withdraw. A second attack by the 15th Warwicks and 2nd KOSBs also failed.

5th Division, Major General Reginald Stephens
13 Brigade, 14th and 15th Warwicks, 2nd KOSBs, 1st Queen's Own
15 Brigade, 16th Warwicks, 1st Norfolks, 1st Bedfords, 1st
    Cheshires
95 Brigade, 1st Devons, 12th Gloucesters, 1st East Surreys, 1st
    DCLI
Pioneers, 1/6th Argylls: Artillery, XV, XVII and XVIII Brigades

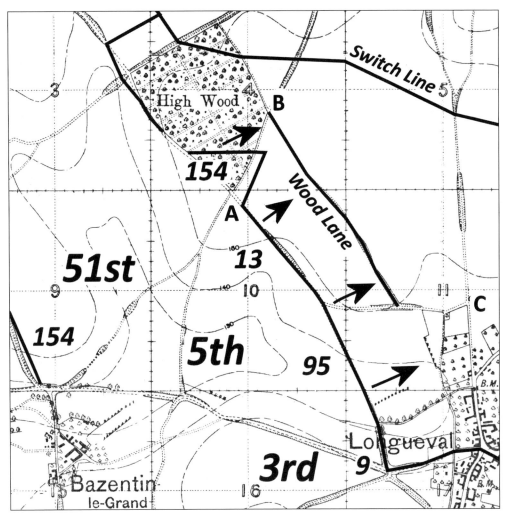

23 July, XV Corps: While 51st Division established a foothold in High Wood, 5th Division could not clear Wood Lane and 3rd Division could not capture the northern end of Longueval.

23 to 30 July, XV Corps' Right

5th Division, Longueval
Viewpoint A: Crucifix, north of Longueval

At 3.20am on 23 July the 1st East Surreys advanced past the north end of Longueval but were then driven back to Pont Street. The 1st DCLIs then had to withdraw from the north end of the village.

Early on 30 July the 14th Warwicks crawled towards the south-east end of Wood Lane, only to be shot down when they charged at 6.10am. The 2nd KOSBs cleared strongpoints at the north end of Longueval and moved into the north-west corner of Delville Wood. Artillery fire forced them to dig in north of the trees and the 1st Queen's Own were unable reinforce them. The 16th Warwicks and the 1st Bedfords took over Longueval and Delville Wood later.

Shelling buried a number of the 1st Norfolks but the survivors advanced through Longueval, into Delville Wood, at 7.10am on 27 July, followed by the 1st Bedfords. The Norfolks made contact with 2nd Division in the centre of the wood and the 16th Warwicks consolidated the west side of the wood; but the north-west corner still could not be secured. The 12th Gloucesters advanced 500 metres north-west of Longueval at 3.30pm on 29 July as the 1st East Surrey cleared the north half of the village.

> 5th Division, Major General Reginald Stephens
> 13 Brigade, 14th Warwicks, 15th Warwicks, 2nd KOSBs, 1st Queen's Own
> 15 Brigade, 16th Warwicks, 1st Norfolks, 1st Bedfords, 1st Cheshires
> 95 Brigade, 1st Devons, 12th Gloucesters, 1st East Surreys, 1st DCLI
> Pioneers, 1/6th Argylls: Artillery, XV, XVII and XVIII Brigades

Memorial B: The 12th Gloucesters (Bristol Own Battalion) memorial is at the junction of the Bazentin-le-Petit and Martinpuich road, west of Longueval

2nd Division, Delville Wood
Viewpoint C: South African memorial

On 27 July the 23rd Royal Fusiliers and 1st KRRC advanced to the north and east edges of Delville Wood as the 1st Berkshires mopped up the centre.

Machine gun fire soon forced the Fusiliers to abandon the north-west corner. German bombers overran six machine gun outposts on the east side of the wood before driving the 1st KRRCs back. Sergeant Albert Gill rallied his men and located snipers until he was killed; he was posthumously awarded the Victoria Cross. The 2nd South Staffords and 17th Middlesex held Delville Wood's centre, while the Germans occupied the east side.

2nd Division, Major General Charles Monro

5 Brigade, 17th Royal Fusiliers, 24th Royal Fusiliers, 2nd Ox and
 Bucks, 2nd HLI

6 Brigade, 1st King's, 2nd South Staffords, 13th Essex, 17th
 Middlesex

99 Brigade, 22nd Royal Fusiliers, 23rd Royal Fusiliers, 1st
 Berkshires, 1st KRRC

Pioneers, 10th DCLI: Artillery, XXXIV, XXXVI and XLI
 Brigades

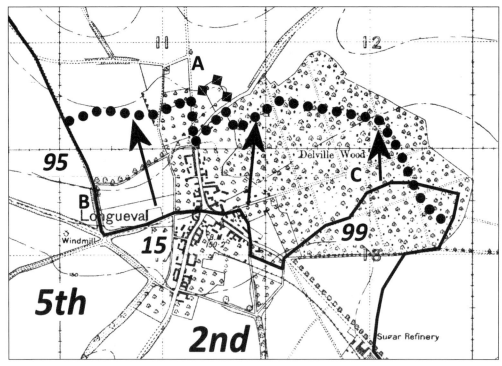

23 to 30 July, XV Corps Right: The attacks failed on 23 July, but 5th Division cleared Longueval and 2nd Division moved north through Delville Wood on 27 July.

23 July, XIII Corps

The 17th Lancashire Fusiliers from 35th Division spent all evening trying to clear the wire between Arrow Head Copse and Maltz Horn Farm because the artillery could not see it.

3rd Division, Delville Wood
Viewpoint A: South African Memorial, Delville Wood
Viewpoint B: Rue de Clos, Trônes Wood road out of Longueval

The artillery failed to fire an intense barrage in front of the 1st Northumberland Fusiliers, so they advanced late and were hit by crossfire from the orchards to the left and Piccadilly to the front. The 13th King's and 12th West Yorkshires lost contact with the Northumberland Fusiliers and were then hit by fire along Piccadilly inside Delville Wood.

The 2nd Royal Scots were delayed because other troops were in their assembly trenches around Waterlot Farm, so they lost the benefit of the barrage as they advanced towards Guillemont station. The 8th East Yorkshires also failed to clear the area south of the railway. They all fell back but stopped a German counter-attack.

3rd Division, Major General Aylmer Haldane
8 Brigade, 2nd Royal Scots, 8th East Yorkshires, 1st Scots Fusiliers, 7th Shropshires
9 Brigade, 1st Northumberland Fusiliers, 4th Royal Fusiliers, 13th King's, 12th West Yorkshires
76 Brigade, 8th King's Own, 2nd Suffolks, 10th Welsh Fusiliers, 1st Gordons
Pioneers, 20th KRRC: Artillery, XXIII, XL, and XLI Brigades

30th Division, Guillemont
Viewpoint C: Guillemont Road Cemetery

Before zero hour smoke bombs fell on the 2nd Green Howards' assembly trenches, north-west of Guillemont. Wind blew the smoke across their front, so they became mixed up with the 8th East Yorkshires on the left and the 19th Manchesters on the right. The Manchesters were shot up getting through the wire covering Guillemont and no runners made it back, so no reinforcements were sent forward. Although the left company withdrew with the Green Howards, the rest of the battalion disappeared.

30th Division, Major General John Shea

21 Brigade, 18th King's Own, 19th Manchesters, 2nd Green
  Howards, 2nd Wiltshires

89 Brigade, 17th King's, 19th King's, 20th King's, 2nd Bedfords

90 Brigade, 16th Manchesters, 17th Manchesters, 18th
  Manchesters, 2nd Scots Fusiliers

Pioneers, 11th South Lancashires: Artillery, CXLVIII, CXLIX,
  CL, CLI Brigades

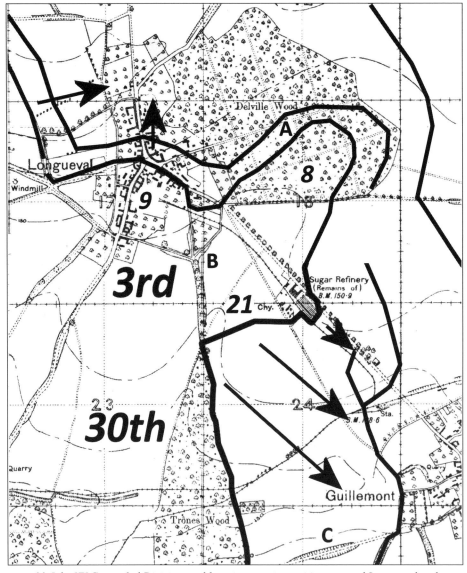

*23 July, XV Corps: 3rd Division could not improve its positions around Longueval and
30th Division failed to reach Guillemont.*

30 July, XIII Corps

2nd Division, Waterlot Farm
Viewpoint A: Rue de Clos, the Trônes Wood road south of Longueval

Machine gun fire stopped the 24th Royal Fusiliers and 2nd Oxford and Bucks advancing far from Waterlot Farm at 4.45am on 30 July. The few Oxford and Bucks who reached Guillemont railway station were captured.

2nd Division, Major General Charles Monro
5 Brigade, 17th Royal Fusiliers, 24th Royal Fusiliers, 2nd Ox and
    Bucks, 2nd HLI
6 Brigade, 1st King's, 2nd South Staffords, 13th Essex, 17th Middlesex
99 Brigade, 22nd Royal Fusiliers, 23rd Royal Fusiliers, 1st
    Berkshires, 1st KRRC
Pioneers, 10th DCLI: Artillery, XXXIV, XXXVI and XLI Brigades

30th Division, Guillemont
Viewpoint B: Guillemont Road Cemetery
Viewpoint C: Pull in before the crucifix by Lonely Trench

Mist delayed the 16th Manchesters and they were stopped by wire between Guillemont station and quarry, so they regrouped in the German front line. The 18th Manchesters cleared the trenches west of Guillemont only to be stopped by crossfire from the station and the quarry. The 2nd Scots Fusiliers advanced into the south-west side of Guillemont and dug in on the north-east side; they would be overrun later. The 16th and 17th Manchesters reinforced a second attack, which also failed.

The 19th King's became disorganised in the mist but some reached the Hardecourt road and the orchards south-east of Guillemont. The 20th King's also reached the Hardecourt road and the 17th King's joined its sister battalions. The 19th King's withdrew from their isolated position early in the afternoon but some dug in along the sunken road. The 2nd Bedfords attacked Maltz Horn Farm with the French and they extended the line from Arrow Head Copse to Maltz Horn Farm.

30th Division, Major General John Shea
21 Brigade, 18th King's Own, 19th Manchesters, 2nd Green
    Howards, 2nd Wiltshires

89 Brigade, 17th King's, 19th King's, 20th King's, 2nd Bedfords
90 Brigade, 16th Manchesters, 17th Manchesters, 18th
    Manchesters, 2nd Scots Fusiliers
Pioneers, 11th South Lancashires: Artillery, CXLVIII, CXLIX,
    CL, CLI Brigades

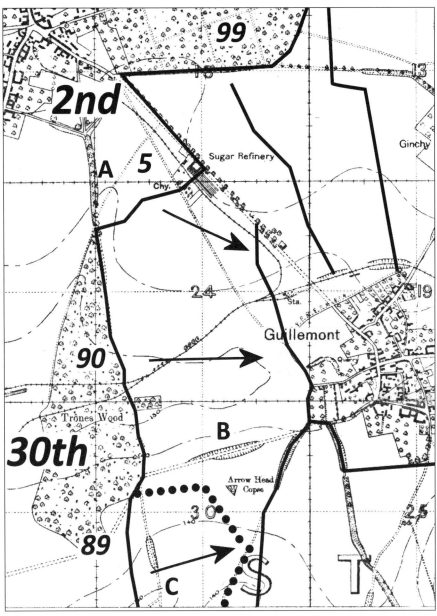

30 July, XIII Corps: While 2nd Division and 30th Division could not reach Guillemont, ground was gained south-west of the village.

3 to 15 August, II Corps

12th (Eastern) Division, west of Pozières

Viewpoint A: Authuille road north from Ovillers, turn to the right, pull in on the left after 200 metres

At 11.15pm on 3 August, the 8th Royal Fusiliers and the 6th Buffs cleared the south-west part of Fourth Avenue and Ration Trench. At 9.15pm on 4 August the 6th Queen's, 6th Queen's Own, 9th Royal Fusiliers, 7th Sussex and 8th Royal Fusiliers cleared most of Ration Trench between the Nordwerk and West Trench. Early on 6 August a flamethrower attack forced the 9th Royal Fusiliers out of Ration Trench. The ends were re-taken but the 7th Suffolks could not take the rest of Ration Trench or West Trench.

At 10.30pm on 12 August the 7th East Surreys and 6th Queen's Own were pinned down in front of Ration Trench. The 9th Essex and 7th Norfolk seized Skyline Trench but it was under heavy shellfire and so they withdrew as many men as possible.

12th (Eastern) Division, Major General Arthur Scott
35 Brigade, 7th Norfolks, 7th Suffolks, 9th Essex, 5th Berkshires
36 Brigade, 8th Royal Fusiliers, 9th Royal Fusiliers, 7th Sussex, 11th Middlesex
37 Brigade, 6th Queen's, 6th Buffs, 7th East Surreys, 6th Queen's Own
Pioneers, 5th Northants: Artillery, LXII, LXIII, LXIV and LXV Brigades

48th (South Midland) Division, Skyline Ridge

Viewpoint A: Authuille road north from Ovillers, turn to the right, pull in on the left after 200 metres

The Germans drove the 1/4th Oxford and Bucks out of Skyline Trench on the night of 13/14 August but they could not take Ration Trench. The 1/4th Berkshires failed to capture the lost ground at dawn but the 1/1st Bucks' bombers cleared it the following night, only to be driven out again by artillery fire.

Attacks by the 1/6th Gloucesters on the evening of 14 August and by the 1/5th Gloucesters, 1/1st Bucks and 1/4th Gloucesters the following afternoon failed to capture Pole Street. Counter-attacks failed to drive the

1/6th Gloucesters back down Nab Valley and the 1/4th Gloucesters also stopped several attacks during the night.

48th (South Midland) Division, Major General Robert Fanshawe
143 Brigade, 1/5th, 1/6th, 1/7th and 1/8th Warwicks
144 Brigade, 1/4th and 1/6th Gloucesters, 1/7th and 1/8th
    Worcesters
145 Brigade, 1/5th Gloucesters, 1/1st and 1/4th Ox & Bucks, 1/4th
    Berkshires
Pioneers, 1/5th Sussex: Artillery, CCXL, CCXLI, CCXLII and
    CCXLIII Brigades

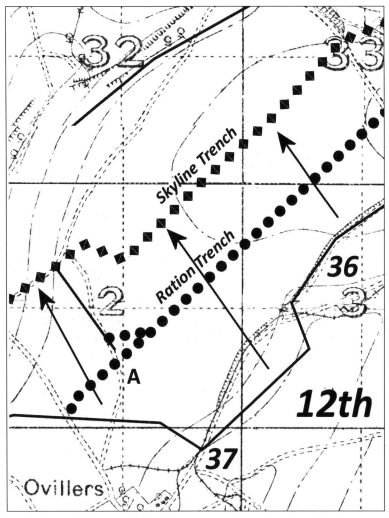

4 to 12 August, II Corps: 12th Division captured Ration Trench and Skyline Trench.

6 to 14 August, I ANZAC Corps

4th Australian Division, Mouquet Farm to Pozières Mill
Viewpoint A: AIF memorial at Mouquet Farm
Viewpoint B: From Pozières civilian cemetery follow the track north to the second bend
Viewpoint C: Pozières windmill

Counter-attacks at dawn on 6 August hit 48th and 14th Australian Battalions north of the Bapaume road. Lieutenant Albert Jacka VC (awarded for deeds in Gallipoli) rounded up many Germans behind 14th Battalion's lines and rescued prisoners by shooting at their guards. The 45th Australian Battalion also stopped a counter-attack south of the Bapaume road.

The 15th Australian Battalion advanced from the trenches north of Pozières cemetery at 9.20pm on 8 August and seized part of Park Lane. At 1am on 9 August 16th Australian Battalion cleared the rest of Park Lane and got close to Mouquet Farm quarry as 13th Battalion reached the OG Trenches, south-east of the farm. During the fighting, Private Martin

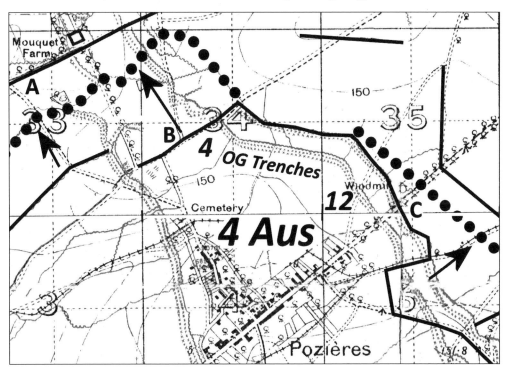

6 to 14 August, I ANZAC Corps: 4th Australian Division struggled to expand the Pozières salient.

O'Meara took ammunition and bombs forward to 16th Battalion and carried wounded men back; he was awarded the Victoria Cross.

Part of 50th Australian Battalion did not receive the order to advance from Ration Trench and Park Lane at 10.30pm on 12 August. The left flank advanced along the Thiepval road but the centre headed towards Mouquet Farm and those who reached the farm had to withdraw. At 10pm on 14 August only a few men of 50th Battalion advanced beyond the quarry and then withdrew. Meanwhile, 13th Australian Battalion veered right to avoid Mouquet Farm and joined 49th Australian Battalion in Fabeck Graben. Machine gun fire stopped 51st Australian Battalion on the right and Fabeck Graben had to be abandoned before dawn.

4th Australian Division, Major General Sir Herbert Cox
4 Brigade, 13th, 14th, 15th and 16th Australian Battalions
12 Brigade, 45th, 46th, 47th and 48th Australian Battalions
13 Brigade, 49th, 50th, 51st and 52nd Australian Battalions
Pioneers, 4th Australian Pioneer Battalion: Artillery, 10th, 11th and
    12th Australian Brigades

The Australian memorial at Pozières Windmill.

4 to 17 August, III Corps

23rd Division, Munster Alley

Viewpoint A: Crossroads with the Martinpuich track on the Pozières to Bazentin road

The 13th Durhams captured part of Munster Alley on the night of 4/5 August but those who reached Torr Trench were killed or captured. On the afternoon of 6 August the 8th Green Howards' bombers cleared more of Torr Trench and Munster Alley. A wounded Private William Short continued to prepare and throw bombs until he died; he was posthumously awarded the Victoria Cross. The 11th West Yorkshires then took over the trench.

23rd Division, Major General James Babington
68 Brigade, 10th North'd Fusiliers, 11th North'd Fusiliers, 12th Durhams, 13th Durhams
69 Brigade, 11th West Yorkshires, 8th Green Howards, 9th Green Howards, 10th Duke's
70 Brigade, 11th Sherwoods, 8th KOYLIs, 8th York and Lancasters, 9th York and Lancasters
Pioneers, 9th South Staffords: Artillery, CII, CIII, CIV and CV Brigades

15th (Scottish) Division, Switch Line

Viewpoint B: Road north of Bazentin-le-Petit, hard-standing on the crest

At 10.30pm on 12 August the 6th Camerons captured the top of Munster Alley and made contact with the Australians. The 12th Highland Light Infantry were pinned down in the centre but the 6/7th Scots Fusiliers reached the trench on the right.

The 7th Camerons captured part of the Switch Line on the morning of 17 August, reinforced by the 8th Seaforths. The 10/11th Highland Light Infantry then extended their hold east of the Elbow.

15th (Scottish) Division, Major General Frederick McCracken
44 Brigade, 9th Black Watch, 8th Seaforths, 10th Gordons, 7th Camerons
45 Brigade, 13th Royal Scots, 6/7th Scots Fusiliers, 6th Camerons, 11th Argylls
46 Brigade, 10th Scottish Rifles, 7/8th KOSBs, 10/11th HLI, 12th HLI

Pioneers, 9th Gordons: Artillery, LXX, LXXI, LXXII and LXXIII
Brigades

1st Division, Intermediate Trench
Viewpoint C: London Cemetery and Extension, High Wood

The 1st Black Watch failed to bomb along Intermediate Trench on the
evening of 16 August; and while the 1st Northants and 2nd Sussex captured
a new trench west of High Wood, they could not hold it. The Black Watch
captured Intermediate Trench at 4.15am the following morning but they had
to withdraw. The problem was the map did not show the whole trench, so
the artillery had not shelled much of it.

1st Division, Major General Peter Strickland
1 Brigade, 10th Gloucesters, 1st Black Watch, 8th Berkshires, 1st
Camerons
2 Brigade, 2nd Sussex, 1st Loyals, 1st Northants, 2nd KRRC
3 Brigade, 1st South Wales Borderers, 1st Gloucesters, 2nd Welsh,
2nd Munsters
Pioneers, 1/6th Welsh: Artillery, XXV, XXVI and XXXIX Brigades

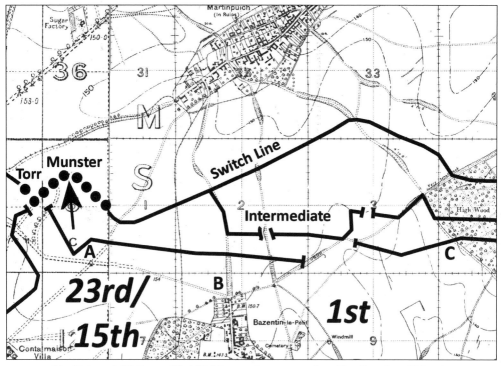

*4 to 17 August, III Corps: 23rd Division made progress along Torr Trench and Munster
Alley but 1st Division could not capture Intermediate Trench.*

8 August, XV Corps

17th (Northern) Division, Longueval and Delville Wood
Viewpoint A: The crucifix north of Longueval
Viewpoint B: South African Memorial

The 9th Northumberland Fusiliers and 12th Manchesters were disorganised by gas and shell fire before their attack at 12.40am on 4 August. Machine guns in Orchard Trench then stopped them. At 4.30pm on 7 August the 8th South Staffords and the 7th Borders were hit by machine gun fire as they emerged from the wood while the British artillery could not see the German trench. The 10th Sherwoods established observation posts north of Longueval during the night.

When 14th Division took over Delville Wood, General Clarke summed up the situation in the wood: 'Conditions were appalling. It was full of gas and corpses; no regular line could be discerned, and the men fought in small groups, mostly in shell holes hastily improvised into fire trenches.' No wonder the men called it Devil's Wood.

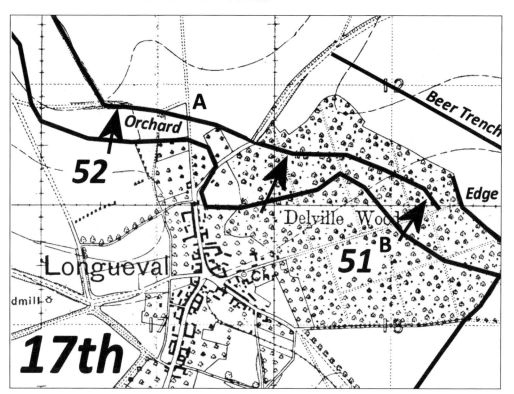

8 August, XV Corps: 17th Division could not advance north of Longueval or through Delville Wood.

17th (Northern) Division, Major General Philip Robertson

50 Brigade, 10th West Yorkshires, 7th East Yorkshires, 7th Green
Howards, 6th Dorsets

51 Brigade, 7th Lincolns, 7th Borders, 8th South Staffords, 10th
Sherwoods

52 Brigade, 9th North'd Fusiliers, 10th Lancashire Fusiliers, 9th
Duke's, 12th Manchesters

Pioneers, 7th York and Lancasters: Artillery, LXXVIII, LXXIX,
LXXX and LXXXI Brigades

Trenches in Longueval and Delville Wood

*Pall Mall led north from Bernafay Wood to the south side of Longueval.
Sloane Street branched to the west, meeting Clarges Street and Pont Street,
and Dover Street branched to the east. Two roads met in the main square
and North Road headed towards Flers with Pont Street north of the village.
Clarges Street ran west from the square with Duke Street running 300 yards
to the north, bounded on the west by Pont Street and Piccadilly on the east.
South Street ran along the south edge of Delville Wood and Prince's Street
ran east from Longueval square through the centre of the wood. The two
were linked by north-south rides called Buchanan Street to the west,
Campbell Street in the centre and King Street to the east. Rotten Row ran
east from Buchanan Street and parallel to Prince's Street. The Strand,
Regent Street and Bond Street, ran north from Prince's Street to the north
edge of the wood.*

Digging trenches through Delville Wood.

8 August, XIII Corps

Six 'Chinese' barrages were used on 7 August, with the barrage intensifying as if zero hour was approaching, and then creeping forward; it then dropped back to catch the Germans manning their parapet.

2nd Division, North-West Guillemont
Viewpoint A: Guillemont Road Cemetery

At 4.20am the 17th Middlesex captured ZZ Trench astride the Longueval road as the 1st King's moved across the German trenches around Guillemont. Many dugouts were missed in the mist, dust and smoke and the Germans reoccupied their trenches and isolated the advancing troops. At 4.20am on 9 August the 17th Middlesex failed to bomb south of Waterlot Farm and the 13th Essex could not reach the German line north-west of Guillemont.

> 2nd Division, Major General Charles Monro
> 5 Brigade, 17th Royal Fusiliers, 24th Royal Fusiliers, 2nd Ox and
>   Bucks, 2nd HLI
> 6 Brigade, 1st King's, 2nd South Staffords, 13th Essex, 17th
>   Middlesex
> 99 Brigade, 22nd Royal Fusiliers, 23rd Royal Fusiliers, 1st
>   Berkshires, 1st KRRC
> Pioneers, 10th DCLI: Artillery, XXXIV, XXXVI and XLI Brigades

55th (West Lancashire) Division, South-West Guillemont
Viewpoint B: The pull-in before the Crucifix near Lonely Trench

The 1/8th King's entered the west side of Guillemont, with the 1/4th Loyals following. The 1/4th King's Own were stopped by wire along the Hardecourt road. The units withdrew in the mist but many of the King's were captured. The 1/5th King's crossed the Hardecourt road only to be pinned down as the 1/6th King's bombers cleared part of Cochrane Alley. Second Lieutenant Gabriel Coury of the 1/4th South Lancashires rescued the wounded Major Swainson from near Arrow Head Copse; he was awarded the Victoria Cross.

The 1/5th Loyals and the 1/10th King's were delayed assembling. The Loyals advanced a few minutes late while the King's had no time to get

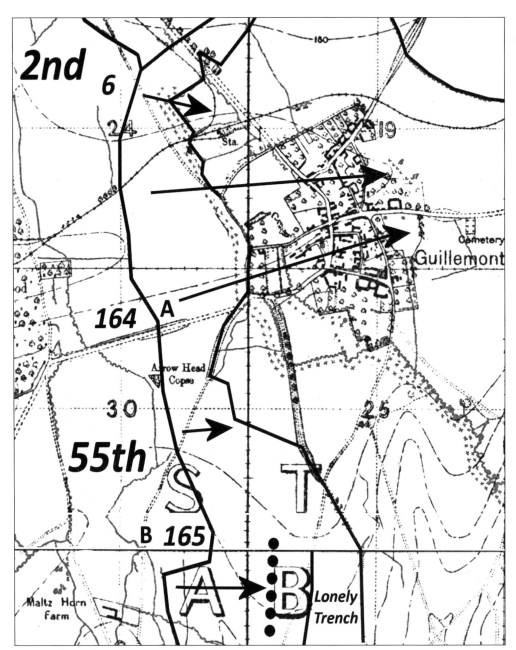

8 August, XIII Corps: While 2nd Division and 55th Division could not capture Guillemont, some ground was gained on the ridge to the south, near Lonely Trench.

their bearings; they were both pinned down in front of wire. The 1/5th King's also failed to improve their position in Cochrane Alley. An injured Captain Noel Chavasse, the 1/10th King's medical officer, spent all day and night searching for wounded; he was awarded his first Victoria Cross (a second was awarded posthumously during the Third Battle of Ypres).

At 5.15pm on 12 August the 1/9th King's advanced towards Lonely Trench and along Cochrane Alley. But the French failed to advance into Maurepas ravine and they withdrew after dusk.

> 55th (West Lancashire) Division, Major General Hugh Jeudwine
> 164 Brigade, 1/4th King's Own, 1/4th Loyals, 1/8th King's, 2/5th Lancashire Fusiliers
> 165 Brigade, 1/5th, 1/6th, 1/7th and 1/9th King's
> 166 Brigade, 1/5th King's Own, 1/10th King's, 1/5th South Lancashires, 1/5th Loyals
> Pioneers, 1/4th South Lancashires: Artillery, CCLXXV, CCLXXVI, CCLXXVII and CCLXXVIII Brigades

Aiming a Stokes mortar.

18 August to 16 September, II Corps

48th (South Midland) Division, Leipzig Salient and Nab Valley
Viewpoint A: Leipzig Salient
Viewpoint B: Authuille road north from Ovillers, turn to the right, stop at the end after 200 metres

On 18 August the 1/5th and 1/6th Warwicks overran the Leipzig Salient as the 1/7th Warwicks' bombers mopped up. The 1/6th Gloucesters bombed towards Pole Trench on 21 August and then at 6pm the 1/4th Gloucesters helped them capture Hindenburg Trench.

The 1/4th Ox and Bucks failed to advance along the east side of Nab valley at 3pm on 23 August because their barrage stopped early. At 7pm on 27 August the 1/5th Gloucesters and 1/4th Berkshires cleared the trench covering Pole Trench. Meanwhile, the 1/8th Warwicks veered to the flanks to avoid their barrage and they could not hold Constance Trench.

    48th (South Midland) Division, Major General Robert Fanshawe
    143 Brigade, 1/5th, 1/6th, 1/7th and 1/8th Warwicks
    144 Brigade, 1/4th and 1/6th Gloucesters, 1/7th and 1/8th
        Worcesters
    145 Brigade, 1/5th Gloucesters, 1/1st and 1/4th Ox & Bucks, 1/4th
        Berkshires
    Pioneers, 1/5th Sussex: Artillery, CCXL, CCXLI, CCXLII and
        CCXLIII Brigades

25th Division, Leipzig Salient
Viewpoint A: Leipzig Salient

At 4.10pm on 25 August the 1st Wiltshires and 3rd Worcesters rushed Hindenburg Trench. At 7pm on 26 August the 8th Loyals captured the west end of Hindenburg Trench but were forced to retire. The 8th South Lancashires failed to capture the same trench at 4pm on 28 August.

At 5.13am on 3 September the 1st Wiltshires, 3rd Worcesters and 2nd South Lancashires captured the trenches either side of the Wonder Work. But no one could enter the Wonder Work and the Wiltshires were forced to withdraw.

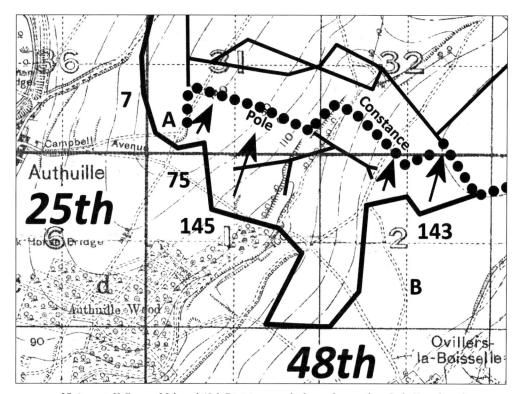

27 August, II Corps: 25th and 48th Divisions worked together to clear Pole Trench and Constance Trench in order to get out of Nab Valley.

25th Division, Major General Guy Bainbridge

7 Brigade, 10th Cheshires, 3rd Worcesters, 8th Loyals, 1st Wiltshires

74 Brigade, 11th Lancashire Fusiliers, 13th Cheshires, 9th Loyals, 2nd Irish Rifles

75 Brigade, 11th Cheshires, 8th Borders, 2nd South Lancashires, 8th South Lancashires

Pioneers, 6th SWBs: Artillery, CX, CXI, CXII and CXIII Brigades

11th (Northern) Division, Skyline Ridge

Viewpoint B: Authuille road north from Ovillers, turn to the right, stop at the end after 200 metres

At 6.30pm on 14 September, the 6th Green Howards, 9th West Yorkshires and the 8th Duke's advanced from Hindenburg Trench. The artillery missed

Turk Trench and the Green Howards suffered heavy casualties but the West Yorkshires entered the Wonder Work. On 16 September the 9th Sherwoods and 6th Lincolns' bombers cleared Constance Trench.

> 11th (Northern) Division, Lieutenant General Sir Charles Woollcombe
>
> 32 Brigade, 9th West Yorkshires, 6th Green Howards, 8th Duke's, 6th York and Lancasters
>
> 33 Brigade, 6th Lincolns, 6th Borders, 7th South Staffords, 9th Sherwoods
>
> 34 Brigade, 8th North'd Fusiliers, 9th Lancashire Fusiliers, 5th Dorsets, 11th Manchesters
>
> Pioneers, 6th East Yorkshires: Artillery, LVIII, LIX and LX Brigades

Going over the top near the Leipzig Salient.

18 to 31 August, I ANZAC Corps

1st Australian Division, North-East of Pozières
Viewpoint A: Pozières windmill

At 9pm on 18 August, 7th Australian Battalion failed to capture a strongpoint south of the Bapaume road. The 8th Australian Battalion advanced three times to the crest but could not cross it. The barrage hit the Australians north of Pozières and while 4th Australian Battalion reached Quarry Trench and the quarry, 3rd Battalion could not capture a new trench in front of Fabeck Graben.

A plan to attack at 6pm on 21 August was interrupted by a German bombardment. A few men from 12th Australian Battalion reached Mouquet Farm but had to withdraw. Although 10th Australian Battalion could not hold onto Fabeck Graben, 11th Australian Battalion eventually linked up the two battalions.

1st Australian Division, Major General Harold Walker
1 (New South Wales) Brigade, 1st, 2nd, 3rd and 4th Australian Battalions
2 (Victoria) Brigade, 5th, 6th, 7th and 8th Australian Battalions
3 Brigade, 9th, 10th, 11th and 12th Australian Battalions
Pioneers, 1st Australian Pioneer Battalion: Artillery, 1st, 2nd and 3rd Australian Brigades

2nd Australian Division, North-West of Pozières
*Viewpoint B: From Pozières civilian cemetery, track north to second bend;
look towards Mouquet Farm*
Viewpoint C: Mouquet Farm, AIF memorial

At 4.45am on 26 August a 22nd Australian Battalion company captured the wrong trench on the left flank and were themselves captured. The 21st Australian Battalion occupied a trench south-west of Mouquet Farm, Zig Zag Trench and the strongpoint at the end of the Mouquet Farm track. But 24th Australian Battalion could not capture Fabeck Graben.

2nd Australian Division, Major General James Legge
5 (New South Wales) Brigade, 17th, 18th, 19th and 20th Australian Battalions

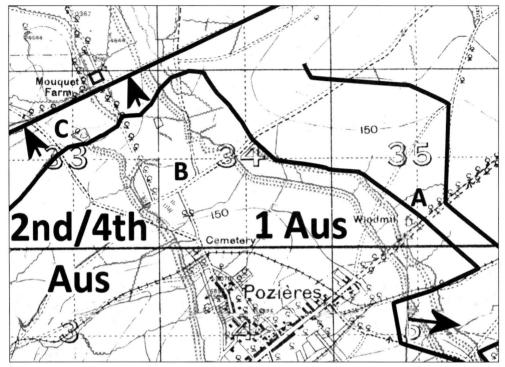

18 to 31 August, I ANZAC Corps: Neither 2nd Australian nor 4th Australian divisions could capture Mouquet Farm; while 1st Australian Division could not advance beyond the OG Trenches

6 (Victoria) Brigade, 21st, 22nd, 23rd and 24th Australian
   Battalions
7 Brigade, 25th, 26th, 27th and 28th Australian Battalions
Pioneers, 2nd Australian Pioneer Battalion: Artillery, 4th, 5th and
   6th Australian Brigades

4th Australian Division, North-West of Pozières
*Viewpoint B: From Pozières civilian cemetery, track north to second bend;
look towards Mouquet Farm*
Viewpoint C: Mouquet Farm, AIF memorial

On the night of 27/28 August, 14th Battalion's bombers captured the
strongpoints at each end of the Mouquet Farm track but the Germans
counter-attacked and few returned. Rain had turned the ground into a
quagmire by the time 16th Battalion tried to take Zig Zag Trench and

Mouquet Farm at 11pm on 29 August. At the same time, 13th Battalion captured Fabeck Graben, east of OG1.

At 5.10am on 3 September 51st Battalion reached Mouquet Farm but many were never seen again. The 52nd and 49th Battalions captured footholds in Fabeck Graben but 52nd Battalion was driven out.

4th Australian Division, Major General Sir Herbert Cox
4 Brigade, 13th, 14th, 15th and 16th Australian Battalions
12 Brigade, 45th, 46th, 47th and 48th Australian Battalions
13 Brigade, 49th, 50th, 51st and 52nd Australian Battalions
Pioneers, 4th Australian Pioneer Battalion: Artillery, 10th, 11th and
    12th Brigades

Australian troops prepare to move up to the front line.

18 to 31 August, III Corps

15th (Scottish) Division, South of Martinpuich and Intermediate Trench
Viewpoint A: Hook Trench, west of High Wood

On 19 August patrols occupied the abandoned Switch Line south of Martinpuich. The 6th Camerons failed to capture Intermediate Trench on 24 August. The 15th Division took over the Intermediate Trench area on the night of 25/26 August and established outposts around the trench by 30 August. Two companies of the 12th Highland Light Infantry were taken prisoner but the surrounded trench garrison eventually gave up.

> 15th (Scottish) Division, Major General Frederick McCracken
> 44 Brigade, 9th Black Watch, 8th Seaforths, 10th Gordons, 7th Camerons
> 45 Brigade, 13th Royal Scots, 6/7th Scots Fusiliers, 6th Camerons, 11th Argylls
> 46 Brigade, 10th Scottish Rifles, 7/8th KOSBs, 10/11th HLI, 12th HLI
> Pioneers, 9th Gordons: Artillery, LXX, LXXI, LXXII Brigade and LXXIII Brigades

1st Division, Intermediate Trench
Viewpoint A: Hard-standing on the track north of Bazentin-le-Petit
Viewpoint B: Hook Trench, west of High Wood

The 1st Black Watch were hit by British and German artillery fire when they left their trench in the thick fog at 4.15am on 18 August. A few men reached Intermediate Trench but they soon withdrew. An attempt at 2.45pm was disrupted when a large-calibre British shell blocked the assembly trench, but 8th Berkshires reached Lancashire Sap, west of High Wood. The 1st Loyals faced the trench at the north-west corner of High Wood. The right company ran into their covering barrage but the left company captured half of the trench and then cleared the rest.

The 1st Northants occupied the abandoned Switch Line, west of High Wood, during the afternoon of 19 August. The 2nd KRRC established an outpost line close to the Switch Line, next to the wood, after dusk. A counter-attack the following morning forced the Northants to withdraw but the 2nd KRRC held on. The Northants and 2nd Sussex failed to retake the

Switch Line at 2.15pm on 20 August. The 2nd Munsters failed to capture Intermediate Trench on 24 August but the 1st SWBs and the Munsters cleared the east end of Intermediate Trench during the night of 26/27 August.

1st Division, Major General Peter Strickland
1 Brigade, 10th Gloucesters, 1st Black Watch, 8th Berkshires, 1st
   Camerons
2 Brigade, 2nd Sussex, 1st Loyals, 1st Northants, 2nd KRRC
3 Brigade, 1st South Wales Borderers, 1st Gloucesters, 2nd Welsh,
   2nd Munsters
Pioneers, 1/6th Welsh: Artillery, XXV, XXVI and XXXIX Brigades

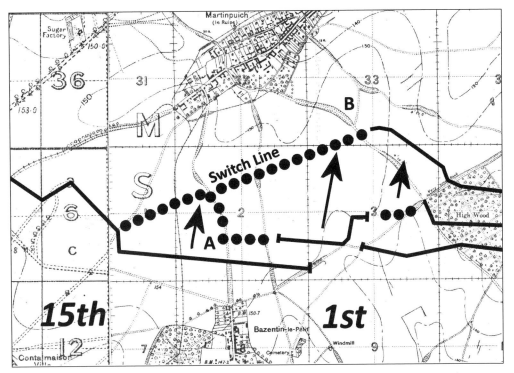

18 to 31 August, III Corps: After a long struggle the Germans withdrew, allowing 15th and 1st Divisions to occupy Intermediate Trench and the Switch Line.

18 to 27 August, XV Corps

33rd Division, High Wood and Wood Lane
Viewpoint A: South corner of High Wood
Viewpoint B: The crucifix north of Longueval

The British artillery fired short and destroyed the flame-throwers while pipe-pushers exploded under the British trench. Livens Projectors fired burning oil at the Switch Line but the Germans shot down the 2nd Argylls when they advanced at 2.45pm.

The smoke bombs failed to create a screen but the 1/4th Suffolks reached Wood Lane under enfilade fire from High Wood. The 4th King's advanced into their own covering barrage and then machine gun teams hiding in shell holes stopped them reaching Wood Lane. The Suffolks then withdrew.

During the night of 20/21 the 1/9th Highland Light Infantry occupied an abandoned Wood Lane east of High Wood; but the 2nd Welsh Fusiliers could not enter the other end of the trench. On 21 August the 8th KRRC failed to drive the Germans out of Delville Wood. A last minute decision was made to capture Orchard Trench at midnight. But the 2nd Worcesters were late and the 1/9th HLI could not advance alone. On 24 August the 1st Queen's bombed along Wood Lane as the 2nd Worcesters and the 16th KRRC captured Tea Trench.

> 33rd Division, Major General Herman Landon
> 98 Brigade, 4th King's, 1/4th Suffolks, 1st Middlesex, 2nd Argylls
> 100 Brigade, 1st Queen's, 2nd Worcesters, 16th KRRC, 1/9th HLI
> 19 Brigade, 20th Royal Fusiliers, 2nd Welsh Fusiliers, 1st Scottish
>   Rifles, 1/5th Scottish Rifles
> Pioneers, 18th Middlesex: Artillery, CLVI, CLXII, CLXVI and
>   CLXVII Brigades

14th (Light) Division, Wood Lane and Delville Wood
Viewpoint B: The crucifix north of Longueval
Viewpoint C: South-east corner of Delville Wood

Machine gun fire stopped the 7th Rifle Brigade's left flank but the right cleared the south end of Wood Lane with the aid of 7th KRRC. Orchard Trench had been obliterated and so the KRRC dug a new trench beyond.

East of Delville Wood, the 6th DCLI were hit by British trench mortar fire and German artillery fire before machine gun fire stopped them reaching Edge Trench. Their bombers captured part of the trench leading to Hop Alley. The 6th Somersets overran Beer Trench, ZZ Trench and part of Hop Alley.

    14th (Light) Division, Major General Victor Couper
    41 Brigade, 7th KRRC, 8th KRRC, 7th Rifle Brigade, 8th Rifle
        Brigade
    42 Brigade, 5th Ox & Bucks, 5th Shropshires, 9th KRRC, 9th Rifle
        Brigade
    43 Brigade, 6th Somersets, 6th DCLI, 6th KOYLIs, 10th Durhams
    Pioneers, 11th King's: Artillery, XLVI, XLVII, XLVIII and XLIX
        Brigades

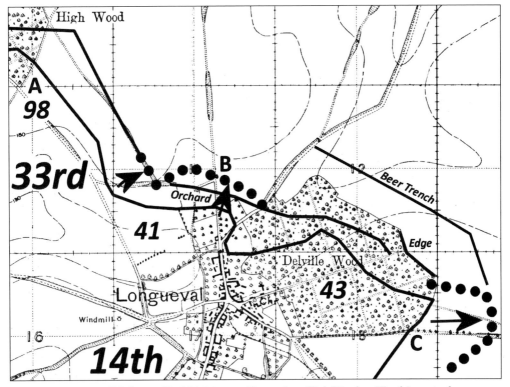

18 August, XV Corps: 33rd Division could not clear High Wood or Wood Lane to the east, whilst 14th Division struggled to extend its hold on Longueval and Delville Wood.

15 to 18 August, XIII and XIV Corps

24th Division, Guillemont and Arrowhead Copse
Viewpoint A: Guillemont Road Cemetery

The 9th East Surrey ran forward from Lamb and New Trenches around Arrowhead Copse at 6pm on 16 August only to be stopped by a shower of grenades. At 2.45pm on 18 August the 8th Buffs captured Machine Gun House and part of ZZ Trench. The 3th Rifle Brigade and 7th Northants cleared trenches west of Guillemont and then came under machine gun fire from Guillemont. They held on with help from the 9th Sussex. The 13th Middlesex faced the same problem south of the road and the German barrage pinned down the support waves in no man's land.

> 24th Division, Major General John Capper
> 17 Brigade, 8th Buffs, 1st Royal Fusiliers, 12th Royal Fusiliers, 3rd Rifle Brigade
> 72 Brigade, 8th Queen's, 9th East Surrey, 8th Queen's Own, 1st North Staffords
> 73 Brigade, 9th Sussex, 7th Northants, 13th Middlesex, 2nd Leinsters
> Pioneers, 12th Sherwoods: Artillery, CVI, CVII, CVIII and CIX Brigades

3rd Division, Lonely Trench
Viewpoint B: Pull in before the crucifix by Lonely Trench

The 12th West Yorkshires and 10th Welsh Fusiliers evacuated their trenches at dusk on 15 August so the heavy artillery could shell Lonely Trench. They crept back when the barrage stopped at 8pm but there was a mix-up over zero hour. The Fusiliers advanced at 10pm and the West Yorkshires scrambled out of their trench and tried to catch up. Only a few reached Lonely Trench. A repeat attack at 4am the following morning failed.

The guns had insufficient time to register and they hit the British trenches on 16 August. The 4th Royal Fusiliers, 13th King's and 8th King's Own could not reach Lonely Trench. The 2nd Suffolks cleared the trench along the Hardecourt road and Cochrane Alley but only to withdraw at dusk.

Crossfire stopped the 8th East Yorkshires south-east of Arrow Head Copse and the 1st Northumberland Fusiliers in front of Lonely Trench. The 10th Welsh Fusiliers overran the south part of Lonely Trench but they soon had to withdraw. Meanwhile, artillery drove the 1st Gordons from Maurepas

Ravine. Early on 19 August the Germans evacuated Lonely Trench and Angle Wood, so the Welsh Fusiliers and Gordons could advance to the next road.

3rd Division, Major General Cyril Deverell
8 Brigade, 2nd Royal Scots, 8th East Yorkshires, 1st Scots Fusiliers, 7th Shropshires
9 Brigade, 1st Northumberland Fusiliers, 4th Royal Fusiliers, 13th King's, 12th West Yorkshires
76 Brigade, 8th King's Own, 2nd Suffolks, 10th Welsh Fusiliers, 1st Gordons
Pioneers, 20th KRRC: Artillery, XXIII, XL, and XLI Brigades

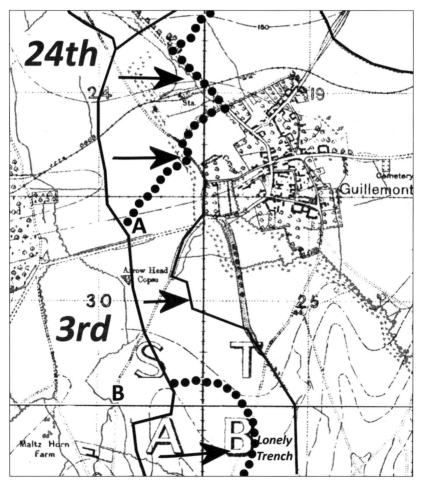

16 to 18 August, XIII Corps: 24th Division closed in on Guillemont from the north-west and 3rd Division occupied Lonely Trench, but only after the Germans abandoned it.

19 to 31 August, XIV Corps

24th Division, Guillemont
Viewpoint A: Guillemont Road Cemetery

A pre-dawn attack on 19 August failed to capture the strongpoint opposite Arrow Head Copse but the 8th Buffs and the 3rd Rifle Brigade discovered ZZ Trench had been abandoned. At 4.30pm the 3rd Rifle Brigade and 1st Royal Fusiliers failed to advance south-east from Guillemont station and the 8th Queen's captured and then lost the quarry.

24th Division, Major General John Capper
17 Brigade, 8th Buffs, 1st Royal Fusiliers, 12th Royal Fusiliers, 3rd Rifle Brigade
72 Brigade, 8th Queen's, 9th East Surreys, 8th Queen's Own, 1st North Staffords
73 Brigade, 9th Sussex, 7th Northants, 13th Middlesex, 2nd Leinsters
Pioneers, 12th Sherwoods: Artillery, CVI, CVII, CVIII and CIX Brigades

20th (Light) Division, Guillemont
Viewpoint A: Guillemont Road Cemetery

On the evening of 23 August, the Germans counter-attacked the 11th KRRC near Guillemont quarry.

20th (Light) Division, Major General William Douglas-Smith
59 Brigade, 10th KRRC, 11th KRRC, 10th Rifle Brigade, 11th Rifle Brigade
60 Brigade, 6th Ox & Bucks, 6th Shropshires, 12th KRRC, 12th Rifle Brigade
61 Brigade, 7th Somersets, 7th DCLI, 7th KOYLIs, 12th King's
Pioneers, 11th Durhams: Artillery, XC, XCI, XCII and XCIII Brigades

35th Division, Arrow Head Copse and Falfemont Farm
Viewpoint B: Pull in before the crucifix by Lonely Trench

Many of the replacements in the 16th Cheshires were 'half grown lads or degenerates'. At 10pm on 21 August they were hit by their own barrage and failed to advance. Most of 35th Division were not ready to attack on the

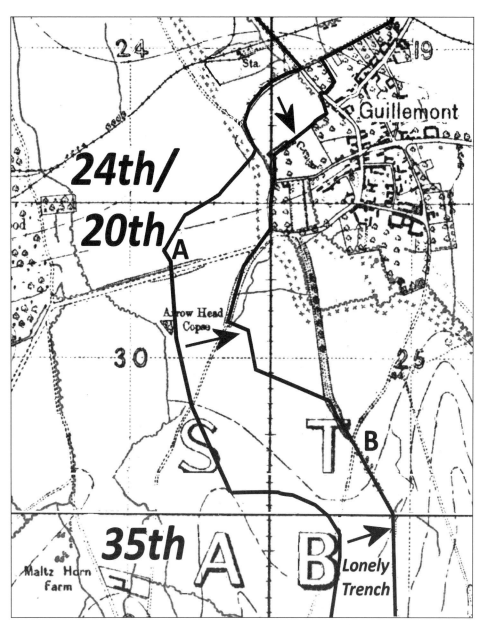

19-31 August, XIV Corps: 24th, 20th and 35th Divisions could not get any closer to Guillemont.

morning of 24 August, so the 17th Lancashire Fusiliers had to advance alone to appease the French, despite protests. They advanced in echelon on the French flank but fell back after the French were driven from the trenches south-east of Falfemont Farm.

> 35th Division, Major General Reginald Pinney (replaced 17 September)
> 104 Brigade, 17th, 18th and 20th Lancashire Fusiliers, 23rd Manchesters
> 105 Brigade, 15th and 16th Cheshires, 14th Gloucesters, 15th Sherwoods
> 106 Brigade, 17th Royal Scots, 17th West Yorkshires, 19th Durhams, 18th HLI
> Pioneers, 19th Northumberland Fusiliers: CLVII, CLVIII, CLVIX, and CLXIII Brigades

Carrying out first aid in the trenches.

27 to 31 August, XV Corps

14th (Light) Division, Delville Wood
Viewpoint A: South-east corner of Delville Wood

At 5.45pm on 24 August the 5th Ox and Bucks, 5th Shropshires and 9th KRRCs cleared part of Beer Trench but machine guns in Ale Alley stopped the 8th KRRC capturing the east end. The Germans then drove the Shropshires and KRRC back into the wood. The 9th Rifle Brigade cleared Edge Trench the following morning. On the afternoon of 27 August the 10th Durhams captured Edge Trench, the final part of Delville Wood. It had taken six weeks to capture all of its 159 acres.

14th (Light) Division, Major General Victor Couper
41 Brigade, 7th KRRC, 8th KRRC, 7th Rifle Brigade, 8th Rifle Brigade
42 Brigade, 5th Ox & Bucks, 5th Shropshires, 9th KRRC, 9th Rifle Brigade
43 Brigade, 6th Somersets, 6th DCLI, 6th KOYLIs, 10th Durhams
Pioneers, 11th King's: Artillery, XLVI, XLVII, XLVIII and XLIX Brigades

24th Division, Counter-attack on Longueval and Delville Wood
Viewpoint B: The crucifix, north of Longueval
Viewpoint C: Side road junction on the north side of the wood

On 31 August the 1st North Staffords and 8th Queen's Own redeployed north of the wood to avoid the German bombardment. The 13th Middlesex were driven out of the west ends of Tea Trench and Orchard Trench but the 9th Sussex and 2nd Leinsters held on to eastern ends. The 2nd Leinsters tried to recapture Orchard Trench but the 3rd Rifle Brigade took it and Wood Lane at 6.30pm.

24th Division, Major General John Capper
17 Brigade, 8th Buffs, 1st Royal Fusiliers, 12th Royal Fusiliers, 3rd Rifle Brigade
72 Brigade, 8th Queen's, 9th East Surreys, 8th Queen's Own, 1st North Staffords
73 Brigade, 9th Sussex, 7th Northants, 13th Middlesex, 2nd Leinsters
Pioneers, 12th Sherwoods: Artillery, CVI, CVII, CVIII and CIX Brigades

7th Division, Counter-attack on Delville Wood
Viewpoint A: South-east corner of Delville Wood

The 1st Welsh Fusiliers and the 10th Durhams cleared part of Ale Alley on 27 and 28 August. On 31 August, Germans wearing khaki uniforms failed to capture Ale Alley and Hop Alley from the 1st South Staffords. A second attack at 7pm forced the Staffords back to Edge Trench. The 2nd Queen's and 1st North Staffords failed to drive them back in the afternoon and on the following day.

> 7th Division, Major General Herbert Watts
> 20 Brigade, 8th and 9th Devons, 2nd Borders, 2nd Gordons
> 22 Brigade, 2nd Warwicks, 2nd Irish Regiment, 1st Welsh
>   Fusiliers, 20th Manchesters
> 91 Brigade, 2nd Queen's, 1st South Staffords, 21st Manchesters,
>   22nd Manchesters
> Pioneers, 24th Manchesters: Artillery, XIV (RHA), XXII and
>   XXXV Brigades

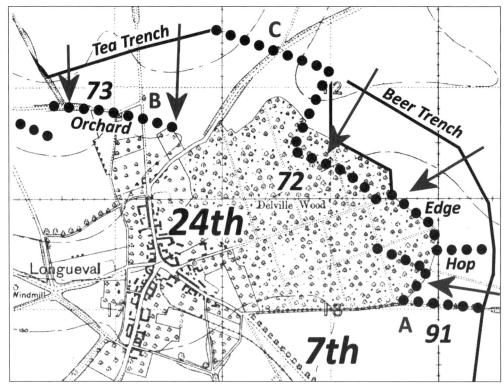

31 August, XV Corps: While 24th Division held onto Longueval, 7th Division held most of Delville Wood during the German counter-attack.

3 September, V Corps

39th Division, West Bank of the Ancre
Viewpoint A: Junction above Hamel

The width of no man's land had been underestimated and the men were still crossing it when the barrage moved forward at 5.10am. It also landed behind one salient, allowing German machine gun teams to stop the 17th Sherwoods. The 16th Rifle Brigade became disorientated in the mist and only a few entered the German trenches alongside the 17th KRRC.

Part of the 14th Hampshires were stopped by wire but the rest crossed the front and support trenches with the 11th Sussex. Everyone had withdrawn to their own trenches by nightfall, despite reinforcements from the 4/5th Black Watch.

39th Division, Major General Gerald Cuthbert
116 Brigade, 11th, 12th and 13th Sussex, 14th Hampshires
117 Brigade, 16th and 17th Sherwoods, 17th KRRC, 16th Rifle Brigade
118 Brigade, 1/6th Cheshires, 1/1st Cambridge, 1/1st Hertfords and 4/5th Black Watch
Pioneers, 13th Gloucesters: Artillery, CLXXIV, CLXXIX, CLXXXIV, CLXXXVI Brigades

49th (West Riding) Division, East Bank of the Ancre
Viewpoint B: Pope's Nose, near St Helen's Tower

Only a few 1/8th West Yorkshires reached the support line next to the river. The 1/6th West Yorkshires were hit by enfilade machine gun fire because wire had stopped the 1/5th Duke's reaching the Pope's Nose, further up the slope. Machine guns in the Strasburg Line stopped the Duke's taking all their objectives. To the rear, Captain William Allen attended to the wounded after a shell hit an ammunition wagon, despite being injured four times himself; he was awarded the Victoria Cross.

The Germans abandoned the St Pierre Divion area by 7.30am, so their machine guns could fire across the river, forcing the rest of 49th Division to withdraw.

49th (West Riding) Division, Major General Edward Perceval
146 Brigade, 1/5th, 1/6th, 1/7th and 1/8th West Yorkshires

147 Brigade, 1/4th, 1/5th, 1/6th and 1/7th Duke's

148 Brigade, 1/4th and 1/5th KOYLIs, 1/4th and 1/5th York &
Lancasters

Pioneers, 19th Lancashire Fusiliers CCXLV, CCXLVI, CCXLVII,
CCXLVIII Brigades

Memorial B: Follow the track to the west of Helen's Tower to the remains of a small concrete and steel girder structure. This was part of the Pope's Nose, an observation post in a small salient in no man's land. There are extensive views across the Ancre valley to Hamel and the Newfoundland Memorial Park.

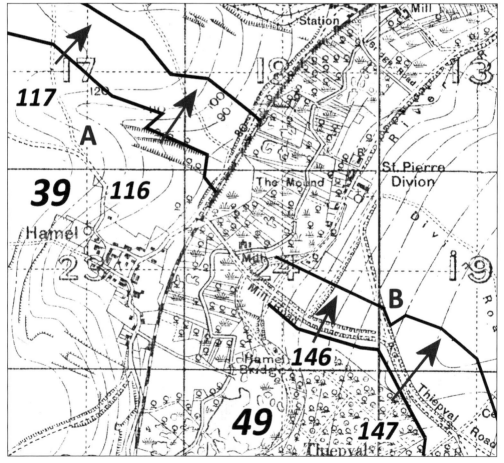

3 September, II Corps: Neither 39th Division nor 49th Division could advance along the banks of the River Ancre.

3 to 10 September, Canadian Corps

Viewpoint A: AIF memorial at Mouquet Farm
Viewpoint B: From Pozières civilian cemetery, track north to second bend;
look towards Mouquet Farm
Viewpoint C: Pozières windmill

1st Canadian Division, Mouquet Farm and Fabeck Graben

The 1st Canadian Division took over the sector on the afternoon of 3
September. Early on 8 September the Germans spotted a relief was
underway and they rushed Fabeck Graben. The 2nd Canadian Battalion
recaptured part of Fabeck Graben at 4.45pm on 9 September and Corporal
Leo Clarke fought to secure the left flank until he was the last man standing.
Clarke then killed nineteen Germans and took the last one prisoner; he was
awarded the Victoria Cross. The 1st Canadian Division was relieved on the
night of 11/12 September, having suffered over 2,800 casualties.

3 to 10 September, Canadian Corps: 1st Canadian Division had a prolonged struggle
for Mouquet Farm and Fabeck Graben.

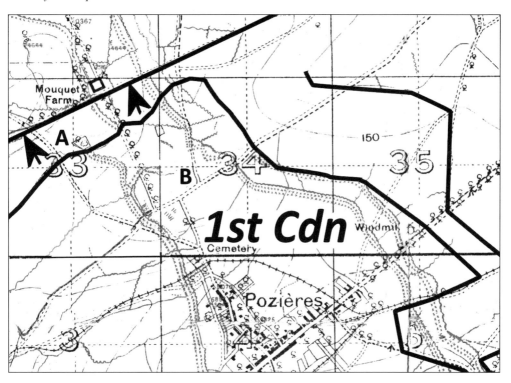

1st Canadian Division, Major General Arthur Currie
1 Brigade, 1st, 2nd, 3rd and 4th Canadian Battalions
2 Brigade, 5th, 7th, 8th and 10th Canadian Battalions
3 Brigade, 13th, 14th, 15th and 16th Canadian Battalions
Pioneers, 1st Canadian Pioneer Battalion: Artillery, 1st, 2nd and 3rd
    Canadian Brigades

The Canadian Corps

*Canadian troops had been in action on the Western Front since April 1915
and they suffered in the first German gas attack north-east of Ypres on 22
April 1915. By the time the Somme ended the Canadian Corps had four
divisions and they were all engaged north of Pozières, capturing Courcelette
with the help of tanks on 15 September. They fought to the north and east of
Courcelette throughout September in a prolonged battle to capture Regina
Trench and again in November. Over 24,000 Canadians were killed or
injured during the battle of the Somme; the missing are remembered on the
Vimy Memorial, north of Arras.*

The Canadian Memorial at Courcelette.

3 to 9 September, III Corps

1st Division, High Wood and Wood Lane
Viewpoint A: London Cemetery and Extension, High Wood

A mine destroyed the strongpoint at the east corner of High Wood thirty seconds before midday on 3 September and the 1st Black Watch's right company captured the crater. The left company suffered casualties when pipe-pushers charges blew back, while Stokes mortar shells fell short and ignited the oil drums. The Black Watch had to re-organise and they were then stopped by machine gun fire. The 1st Camerons captured Wood Lane to the south-east but an 8th Berkshires' detachment could not cross no man's land on the right. The Germans soon drove the Black Watch from the crater and then fired at the Camerons until they withdrew.

An attempt to clear the wood at 6pm on 8 September was disrupted when the British barrage hit the 1st Gloucesters. German artillery and machine gun fire then stopped the battalion advancing along the west side of the wood and it eventually withdrew back to New Trench. The 2nd Welsh's left company could not clear the western perimeter of the wood but the right company reached the Switch Line inside it.

At 4.45pm on 9 September the 10th Gloucesters advanced through the north-west corner of High Wood but machine gun fire from the Switch Line forced them to retire. A mine was blown under the strongpoint at the east corner of the wood thirty seconds before zero and the 1st Northants captured the crater. The 2nd Munsters and Northants could not capture the Switch Line but the 2nd Sussex and 2nd KRRC captured Wood Lane to the east.

1st Division, Major General Peter Strickland
1 Brigade, 10th Gloucesters, 1st Black Watch, 8th Berkshires, 1st Camerons
2 Brigade, 2nd Sussex, 1st Loyals, 1st Northants, 2nd KRRC
3 Brigade, 1st South Wales Borderers, 1st Gloucesters, 2nd Welsh, 2nd Munsters
Pioneers, 1/6th Welsh Regiment: Artillery, XXV, XXVI and XXXIX Brigades

Memorial B: The 1st Camerons have a memorial on the eastern edge of High Wood; the 1st Black Watch are commemorated by an inscription on its rear.

15th (Scottish) Division, Intermediate Trench, 4 to 8 September
Viewpoint C: Hook Trench hard-standing, west of High Wood.

At 6pm on 8 September the 9th Black Watch and 1st Gloucesters captured Intermediate Trench west of High Wood. But first the Gloucesters and then the Black Watch had to fall back.

> 15th (Scottish) Division, Major General Frederick McCracken
> 44 Brigade, 9th Black Watch, 8th Seaforths, 10th Gordons, 7th Camerons
> 45 Brigade, 13th Royal Scots, 6/7th Scots Fusiliers, 6th Camerons, 11th Argylls
> 46 Brigade, 10th Scottish Rifles, 7/8th KOSBs, 10/11th HLI, 12th HLI
> Pioneers, 9th Gordons: Artillery, XXV, XXVI, XXXIX and LXI Brigades

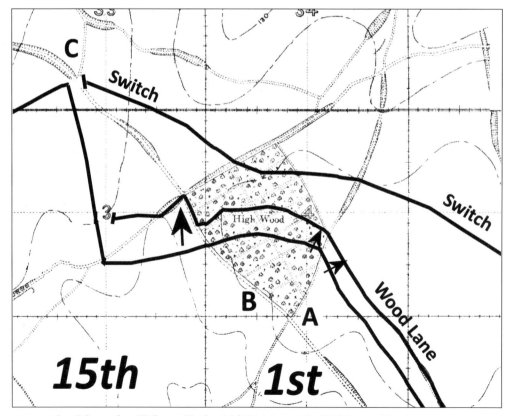

3 to 9 September, III Corps: Neither 15th Division nor 1st Division could make progress in the High Wood area.

3 September, XV Corps

24th Division, Longueval and Delville Wood
Viewpoint A: Crucifix north of Longueval

The 8th Buffs first attack at midday from Orchard Trench was late because the runners were killed. A second attack at 4pm failed because the covering artillery barrage did not creep forward at zero hour. Meanwhile, the 7th Northants captured Tea Lane east of North Street.

> 24th Division, Major General John Capper
> 17 Brigade, 8th Buffs, 1st Royal Fusiliers, 12th Royal Fusiliers, 3rd Rifle Brigade
> 72 Brigade, 8th Queen's, 9th East Surrey, 8th Queen's Own, 1st North Staffords
> 73 Brigade, 9th Sussex, 7th Northants, 13th Middlesex, 2nd Leinsters
> Pioneers, 12th Sherwoods: Artillery, CVI, CVII, CVIII and CIX Brigades

7th Division, Ginchy
Viewpoint B: South-east corner of Delville Wood

The 2nd Queen's advanced along the south-east edge of Delville Wood at midday but the smoke from their fumite grenades disclosed their location and they were unable to reach Hop Alley. The 9th East Surreys' attack towards Ale Alley was cancelled due to a mix-up over orders.

The 1st Welsh Fusiliers crept across no man's land and captured the south end of Beer Trench but the men who entered the north part of Ginchy were never seen again. The 2nd Warwicks were unable to reach Ale Alley but the 20th Manchesters cleared Waterlot Farm and the south half of Ginchy.

At 2.15pm the 2nd Irish Regiment tried and failed to extend the left flank. The Manchesters were then driven from Ginchy, taking some of the Irishmen and Warwicks with them, but the rest of the Warwicks held onto the south-west corner of the village. The Irishmen were unable to capture Hop Alley or re-occupy Ginchy and the Germans had soon re-entered the village.

7th Division, Major General Herbert Watts

20 Brigade, 8th Devons, 9th Devons, 2nd Borders, 2nd Gordons

22 Brigade, 2nd Warwicks, 2nd Irish Regiment, 1st Welsh Fusiliers, 20th Manchesters

91 Brigade, 2nd Queen's, 1st South Staffords, 21st Manchesters, 22nd Manchesters

Pioneers, 24th Manchesters: Artillery, XIV, XXII and XXXV Brigades

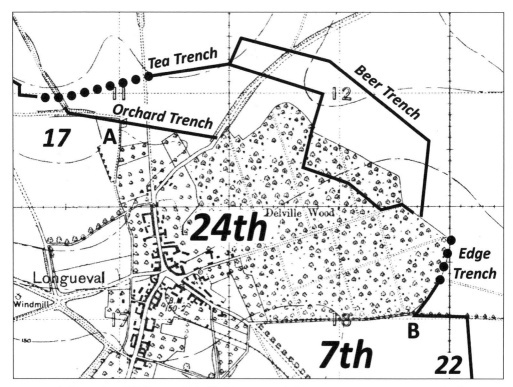

3 September, XV Corps: 24th Division struggled to improve its position north of Longueval while 7th Division did the same around Delville Wood.

3 September, XIV Corps

20th (Light) Division, Guillemont

Viewpoint A: Guillemont Road Cemetery
Viewpoint B: 20th (Light) Division memorial

At noon the 7th Leinsters advanced past Guillemont station and Lieutenant John Holland captured fifty prisoners; he was awarded the Victoria Cross. The 6th Connaughts entered Guillemont but failed to clear the quarry and came under fire from the rear. A wounded Private Thomas Hughes captured the machine gun holding up his company; he was awarded the Victoria Cross. The 10th KRRC's reserve company cleared the quarry and the rest of the battalion joined the 10th and 11th Rifle Brigade along the Hardecourt road, south-west of the village.

The 12th King's dug in on the north side of Guillemont, where Sergeant David Jones would fight off counter-attacks for two days; he was awarded the Victoria Cross. The 8th Munsters advanced to North Street while the 6th Oxford and Bucks and 7th Somersets reached South Street. A mixture of units met few Germans when they advanced east at 2.50pm. The Germans counter-attacked through Leuze Wood and then abandoned the wood. The 7th Somersets established posts between the Guillemont Road and the west corner of Leuze Wood on 4 September.

20th (Light) Division, Major General William Douglas-Smith
59 Brigade, 10th and 11th KRRC, 10th and 11th Rifle Brigade
60 Brigade, 6th Ox & Bucks, 6th Shropshires, 12th KRRC, 12th Rifle Brigade
61 Brigade, 7th Somersets, 7th DCLI, 7th KOYLIs, 12th King's
Pioneers, 11th Durhams: Artillery, XC, XCI, XCII and XCIII Brigades

Memorial B: The 20th (Light) Division memorial is east of Guillemont, on the Combles road. The original memorial obelisk/pillar had to be demolished as it had become unstable. The commemorative plaque was placed on a new plinth.

5th Division, Wedge Wood and Falfemont Farm

Viewpoint A: Guillemont Road Cemetery
Viewpoint B: 20th (Light) Division memorial

The 2nd KOSBs were shot down whilst advancing towards Falfemont Farm at 8.50am; it looked as though 'they had been mown down on parade'. At midday the 1st DCLI and 12th Gloucesters captured the trenches south of Guillemont. The Gloucesters then captured the trenches south-east of Guillemont, under fire from Falfemont Farm. The advance ended at the sunken track which ran into Wedge Wood ravine.

The barrage landed behind the 14th and 15th Warwicks and, while they cleared Wedge Wood ravine, they could not reach Falfemont Farm. At 6.30pm the 1st Bedfords cleared Wedge Wood but the 1st Cheshires still could not take Falfemont Farm.

5th Division, Major General Reginald Stephens
13 Brigade, 14th and 15th Warwicks, 2nd KOSBs, 1st Queen's Own
15 Brigade, 16th Warwicks, 1st Norfolks, 1st Bedfords, 1st
    Cheshires
95 Brigade, 1st Devons, 12th Gloucesters, 1st East Surreys, 1st DCLI
Pioneers, 1/6th Argylls: Artillery, XV, XVII and XVIII Brigades

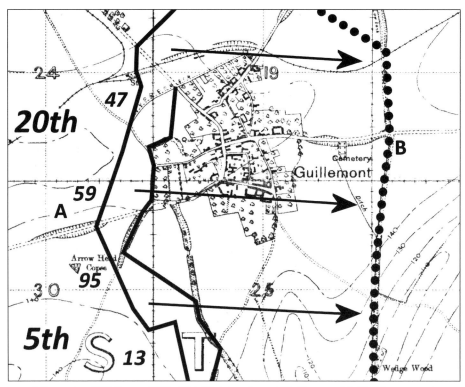

3 September, XIV Corps: While 20th Division cleared Guillemont, 5th Division crossed the valley to the south.

4 to 8 September, XV Corps

55th (West Lancashire) Division, Delville Wood
Viewpoint A: The crucifix north of Longueval
Viewpoint B: Junction on the Flers road, north of Delville Wood

On the night of 5/6 September the 1/6th King's bombers failed to clear Wood Lane but the 1/7th King's occupied an abandoned Tea Trench. The Germans also withdrew from Beer Trench. Two nights later the 1/5th King's occupied the south end of Wood Lane, north-west of Longueval.

> 55th (West Lancashire) Division, Major General Hugh Jeudwine
> 164 Brigade, 1/4th King's Own, 1/4th Loyals, 1/8th King's, 2/5th
>   Lancashire Fusiliers
> 165 Brigade, 1/5th, 1/6th, 1/7th and 1/9th King's
> 166 Brigade, 1/5th King's Own, 1/10th King's, 1/5th South
>   Lancashires, 1/5th Loyals
> Pioneers, 1/4th South Lancashires: Artillery, CCLXXV, CCLXXVI,
>   CCLXXVII and CCLXXVIII Brigades

7th Division, Ginchy
Viewpoint C: South-east corner of Delville Wood

Ginchy was not shelled because it was thought British troops might be holding it. Consequently the 9th Devons' attack at 8am on 4 September was a disaster. The 21st Manchesters' advance at 2pm failed to reach Ale Alley or Hop Alley. The 2nd Queen's advanced towards the east corner of Delville Wood at 5.30pm but the trench mortars could not knock out the German machine guns.

Plans for a surprise night attack against Ginchy never materialised because the 8th Devons arrived late while the 2nd Gordons lost all their officers before zero hour. The 2nd Queen's captured the south-east corner of Delville Wood at 3.30am on 5 September and were reinforced by the 8th Devons.

The Gordons advanced towards Ginchy at 5am on 6 September, only they went in the wrong direction. They returned to their start line and advanced the right way but still could not reach Ginchy. A repeat attack with the 9th Devons on their right was made at 2pm. The Gordons entered Ginchy but reinforcements could not reach them and they were soon forced out.

7th Division, Major General Herbert Watts

20 Brigade, 8th Devons, 9th Devons, 2nd Borders, 2nd Gordons

22 Brigade, 2nd Warwicks, 2nd Irish Regiment, 1st Welsh Fusiliers, 20th Manchesters

91 Brigade, 2nd Queen's, 1st South Staffords, 21st Manchesters, 22nd Manchesters

Pioneers, 24th Manchesters: Artillery, XIV, XXII and XXXV Brigades

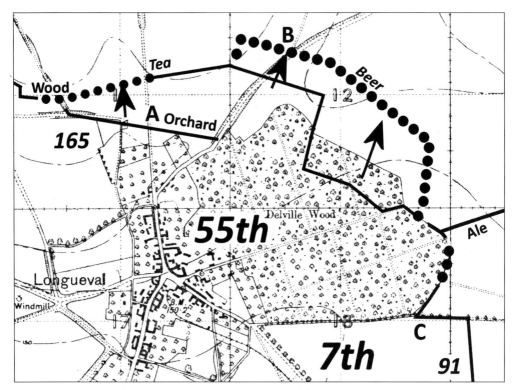

4 to 8 September, XV Corps: 55th Division occupied the ground north of Delville Wood after the Germans withdrew towards Flers.

4 to 8 September, XIV Corps

5th Division, Falfemont Farm and Leuze Wood
Viewpoint A: 20th (Light) Division memorial, east of Guillemont

At 3.10pm on 4 September, the 1st Bedfords bombed from Wedge Wood to the north-west corner of Falfemont Farm. The 1st Norfolks could not reach the opposite corner of the farm because the French had not moved in Combles ravine. A company of the 1st Cheshires reached the far side of the spur, where they were reinforced by the 16th Warwicks. Wire hidden in the corn in front of Combles Trench stopped the 7th Irish Fusiliers reaching the Warwicks.

The 1st East Surreys occupied Valley Trench at 6.30pm on 4 September. The British barrage stopped the 1st Devons entering Leuze Wood until the artillery observers lengthened the range. The 1st Norfolks eventually captured Falfemont Farm and nearby Point 48 at 3am on 5 September. At

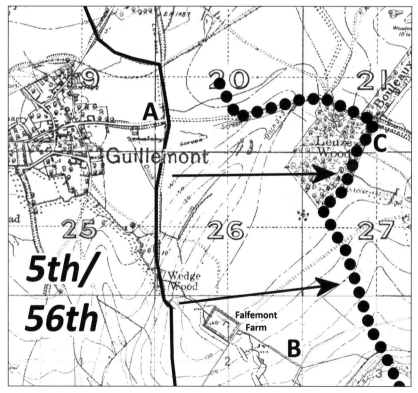

4 to 8 September, XIV Corps: 5th Division captured Falfemont Farm and then occupied Leuze Wood before 56th Division secured the position.

8.30am the 16th Warwicks dug in along the adjacent slope and the 1st Devons moved through the rest of Leuze Wood during the afternoon.

5th Division, Major General Reginald Stephens
13 Brigade, 14th Warwicks, 15th Warwicks, 2nd KOSBs, 1st Queen's Own
15 Brigade, 16th Warwicks, 1st Norfolks, 1st Bedfords, 1st Cheshires
95 Brigade, 1st Devons, 12th Gloucesters, 1st East Surreys, 1st DCLI
Pioneers, 1/6th Argylls: Artillery, XV, XVII and XVIII Brigades

56th (1st London Division) Division, Leuze Wood
Viewpoint B: Hard-standing south-west of Falfemont, on the Combles to Maurepas Road
Viewpoint C: Guillemont to Combles road, east side of Leuze Wood

The 56th Division took over from the 5th Division on 7 September. The Germans, seeing the relief taking place, drove the 13th and 14th Londons back into Leuze Wood. The Londoners recovered the lost ground before nightfall. The 1/5th London captured and then lost Combles Trench.

56th (1st London) Division, Major General Charles Hull
167 Brigade, 1/1st London, 1/3rd London, 1/7th and 1/8th Middlesex
168 Brigade, 1/4th, 1/12th, 1/13th and 1/14th London
169 Brigade, 1/2nd, 1/5th, 1/9th and 1/16th London
Pioneers, 1/5th Cheshires: Artillery, CCLXXX, CCLXXXI, CCLXXXII and CCLXXXIII Howitzer Brigades

Carrying ammunition forward.

9 September, XV Corps and XIV Corps' Left

55th (West Lancashire) Division, Wood Lane
Viewpoint A: The crucifix north of Longueval
Viewpoint B: South-east corner of Delville Wood

The 1/5th and 1/6th King's bombed from Orchard Trench into Wood Lane. The 1/4th Loyals captured the trenches east of Delville Wood, the 2/5th Lancashire Fusiliers captured a trench later called the Haymarket and the 1/5th King's bombed along Ale Alley. Two days later the 1/4th King's Own failed to take Hop Alley.

> 55th (West Lancashire) Division, Major General Hugh Jeudwine
> 164 Brigade, 1/4th King's Own, 1/4th Loyals, 1/8th King's, 2/5th Lancashire Fusiliers
> 165 Brigade, 1/5th, 1/6th, 1/7th and 1/9th King's
> 166 Brigade, 1/5th King's Own, 1/10th King's, 1/5th South Lancashires, 1/5th Loyals
> Pioneers, 1/4th South Lancashires: Artillery, CCLXXV, CCLXXVI, CCLXXVII and CCLXXVIII Brigades

16th (Irish) Division, Ginchy
Viewpoint C: Crucifix north edge of Guillemont

The 7th Irish Fusiliers and 7th Irish Rifles advanced astride the Delville Wood road into the south-west corner of Ginchy. The 9th and 8th Dublin Fusiliers then cleared the rest of the village. Machine gun fire stopped the 8th Munsters and the 6th Irish Regiment advancing south-east of Ginchy while the 6th Connaught Rangers veered south, rather than towards the Quadrilateral.

> 16th (Irish) Division, Major General William Hickie
> 47 Brigade, 6th Irish Regiment, 6th Connaughts, 7th Leinsters, 8th Munsters
> 48 Brigade, 7th Irish Rifles, 1st Munsters, 8th and 9th Dublin Fusiliers
> 49 Brigade, 7th and 8th Inniskillings, 7th and 8th Irish Fusiliers
> Pioneers, 11th Hampshires: Artillery, LXXVII, CLXXVII and CLXXX Brigades

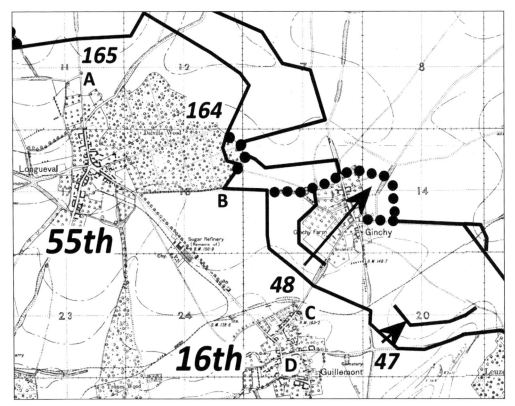

9 September, XV Corps Right and XIV Corps Left: On 9 September, 55th Division improved its position around Delville Wood as the 16th Division captured Ginchy; the Guards Division then secured the village.

Memorial D: The 16th (Irish) Division's memorial is in front of Guillemont church.

Guards Division, Ginchy
Viewpoint C: Crucifix north edge of Guillemont

On 10 September the Germans pushed through the Welsh Guards in the mist and entered the north-east side of Ginchy; they were soon forced out. The 1st Grenadier Guards then reinforced the Welsh Guards and the 4th Grenadier Guards. The Grenadiers advanced east of Ginchy on 12 September and later that evening cleared the re-entrant east of the village with the 2nd Scots Guards. The following evening the 2nd Grenadier

Guards straightened the line north of Ginchy but the 2nd Irish Guards could not reach the trench north of the Quadrilateral.

Guards Division, Major General Geoffrey Feilding
1 Brigade, 2nd Grenadier Guards, 2nd and 3rd Coldstream Guards, 1st Irish Guards
2 Brigade, 3rd Grenadier Guards, 1st Coldstream Guards, 1st Scots Guards, 2nd Irish Guards
3 Brigade, 1st and 4th Grenadier Guards, 2nd Scots Guards, 1st Welsh Guards
Pioneers, 4th Coldstream Guards: Artillery, LXI, LXXIV, LXXV and LXXVI Brigade RFA

Stretcher bearers cross the battlefield.

9 September, XIV Corps' Right

56th (1st London) Division, the Quadrilateral
Viewpoint A: 20th Division memorial at the crossroads east of Guillemont
Viewpoint B: The Quadrilateral

Zero hour was set for 4.45pm but the 1/12th London advanced late, missed the barrage and were pinned down by the Quadrilateral. The 1/4th London reached the trench between the Quadrilateral and Bouleaux Wood and the 1/13th London moved up in support. The British heavy artillery hit the 1/9th and 1/5th London while the creeping barrage was 'practically non-existent'. The 1/9th London captured a trench inside Bouleaux Wood but the 1/5th London could not reach Loop Trench, in spite of help from the 1/2nd London.

The 1/16th London advanced through mist out of Leuze Wood at 7am the following morning only to be shot down by the machine gun teams in Loop Trench and along the Combles road. A second attempt at 3pm by the 1/2nd London also failed. The 1/14th London lost direction at 12.15am and found themselves in the trench south-east of the Quadrilateral. The 1/8th Middlesex stopped counter-attacks from Bouleaux Wood on 11 September.

> 56th (1st London) Division, Major General Charles Hull
> 167 Brigade, 1/1st London, 1/3rd London, 1/7th and 1/8th Middlesex
> 168 Brigade, 1/4th, 1/12th, 1/13th and 1/14th London
> 169 Brigade, 1/2nd, 1/5th, 1/9th and 1/16th London
> Pioneers, 1/5th Cheshires: Artillery, CCLXXX, CCLXXXI, CCLXXXII and CCLXXXIII Howitzer Brigades

Memorial C: Major Cedric Charles Dickens was killed trying to establish contact with the Irishmen on the Londoners' left. He was the grandson of the prolific Victorian author Charles Dickens. A cross was placed over what was believed to be his grave; later investigation could not find the body and the cross was moved a few hundred yards to a more accessible location. He is commemorated on the Thiepval Memorial.

6th Division, Quadrilateral
Viewpoint B: The Quadrilateral

At 6am and 6pm on 13 September machine gun fire stopped the 2nd Sherwoods and the 9th Suffolks reaching the Quadrilateral.

6th Division, Major General Charles Ross

16 Brigade, 1st Buffs, 8th Bedfords, 1st Shropshires, 2nd York and Lancasters

18 Brigade, 1st West Yorkshires, 11th Essex, 2nd Durhams, 14th Durhams

71 Brigade, 9th Norfolks, 9th Suffolks, 1st Leicesters, 2nd Sherwoods

Pioneers, 11th Leicesters: Artillery, II, XXIV, XXXVIII Brigades

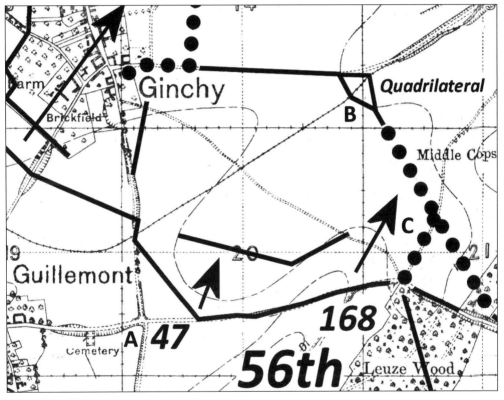

9 September, XIV Corps Right: 56th Division advanced north of Leuze Wood but could not reach the Quadrilateral.

15 to 22 September, Canadian Corps

3rd Canadian Division, Mouquet Farm, Zollern Graben and Zollern Redoubt
Viewpoint A: Mouquet Farm, AIF memorial

On 15 September the 1st Canadian Mounted Rifles (CMRs) raided Mouquet Farm but they could not reach Zollern Redoubt. The 5th CMRs blocked the trench linked to Fabeck Graben. The 4th CMRs cleared the west end of Fabeck Graben after 2nd Canadian Division cleared the east end.

At 5pm on 16 September the barrage missed Zollern Graben and the 42nd Canadian Battalion and the Royal Canadian Regiment were halted. Private John Kerr of the 49th Canadian Battalion captured sixty-two prisoners and 250 metres of Fabeck Graben; he was awarded the Victoria Cross. The Princess Patricia's Canadian Light Infantry held on in Fabeck Graben.

The 58th Canadian Battalion bombed along the trenches and 43rd Canadian Battalion went over the top at 5am on 20 September. They captured part of Zollern Graben but the Germans retook it at their fifth counter-attack.

> 3rd Canadian Division, Major General Louis Lipsett
> 7 Brigade, Princess Patricia's, Royal Canadian Regiment, 42nd and 49th Canadian Battalions
> 8 Brigade, 1st, 2nd, 4th and 5th Canadian Mounted Rifles (CMRs)
> 9 Brigade, 43rd, 52nd, 58th and 60th Canadian Battalions
> Pioneers, 3rd Canadian Pioneer Battalion: Artillery, 8th, 9th, 10th and 11th Artillery Brigades

2nd Canadian Division, Courcelette
Viewpoint B: Pozières Windmill
Viewpoint C: Courcelette British Cemetery
Viewpoint D: Courcelette civilian cemetery
Viewpoint E: Canadian Courcelette Memorial

One tank broke down but two others accompanied 28th Canadian Battalion at 6.20am to McDonnell Trench until they ditched. One tank ditched early but two others helped 21st Canadian Battalion capture the Sugar Factory. The 20th Canadian Battalion reached Gun Pit Trench on the outskirts of Courcelette before withdrawing to its objective; 18th Canadian Battalion then came under fire from Factory Lane. At 9.20am 21st and 20th Canadian Battalions advanced to Courcelette while 18th Canadian Battalion occupied the sunken road next to Gun Pit Trench.

At 6pm 42nd Canadian Battalion captured part of Fabeck Graben but the Princess Patricia's captured McDonnell by mistake before taking the east end of Fabeck Graben. The 25th Canadian Battalion cleared the north side of Courcelette and the 22nd Canadian Battalion cleared the south side as the 26th Canadian Battalion mopped up. At 5pm on 17 September, 5 Brigade failed to capture the trenches east of Courcelette.

2nd Canadian Division, Major General Richard Turner
4 Brigade, 18th, 19th, 20th and 21st Canadian Battalions
5 Brigade, 22nd, 24th, 25th and 26th Canadian Battalions
6 Brigade, 27th, 28th, 29th and 31st Canadian Battalions
Pioneers, 2nd Canadian Pioneer Battalion: Artillery, 4th, 5th, 6th
   and 7th Canadian Brigades

Memorial B: The tank memorial stands alongside the Bapaume road, northeast of Pozières (opposite the Australian memorial). Three tanks crawled down the road towards Courcelette with Canadian troops on 15 September.

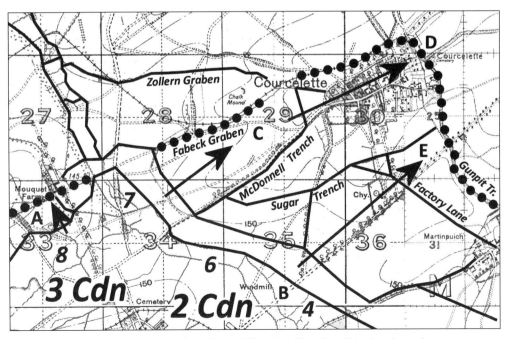

15 to 22 September, Canadian Corps: While 3rd Canadian Division drew closer to Mouquet Farm, tanks helped 2nd Canadian Division capture Courcelette.

15 September, III Corps

15th (Scottish) Division, Martinpuich
Viewpoint A: Courcelette Canadian memorial

A tank helped the 10th/11th HLI and the 7th/8th KOSBs reach the Courcelette–Martinpuich road as the 10th Scottish Rifles cleared Martinpuich. The 13th Royal Scots and 11th Argylls cleared Tangle Trench before advancing to the Longueval road. Later the 12th HLI and the 9th York and Lancasters occupied Martinpuich, while the 6th Camerons occupied Prue Trench.

> 15th (Scottish) Division, Major General Frederick McCracken
> 44 Brigade, 9th Black Watch, 8th Seaforths, 10th Gordons, 7th Camerons
> 45 Brigade, 13th Royal Scots, 6/7th Scots Fusiliers, 6th Camerons, 11th Argylls
> 46 Brigade, 10th Scottish Rifles, 7/8th KOSBs, 10/11th HLI, 12th HLI
> Pioneers, 9th Gordons: Artillery, LXX, LXXI, LXXII Brigade and LXXIII Brigades

50th (Northumbrian) Division, the Starfish Line
Viewpoint B: Hook Trench, west of High Wood

Two tanks helped the 1/5th and 1/4th Green Howards, and 1/4th East Yorkshires overran Hook Trench. One tank was disabled but the second cleared Martin Trench and the Starfish Line. The 1/7th and 1/4th Northumberland Fusiliers crossed Hook Trench and reached the Starfish Line and the Switch Line while the 1/6th Northumberland Fusiliers formed a flank facing High Wood.

Artillery fire forced a withdrawal to Martin Alley, Martin Trench and Hook Trench. The 1/9th and 1/6th Durhams were stopped trying to retake Hook Trench at 9.40pm. The 1/5th Borders' guides got lost and their 11pm advance was pinned down.

> 50th (Northumbrian) Division, Major General Percival Wilkinson
> 149 Brigade, 1/4th, 1/5th, 1/6th and 1/7th Northumberland Fusiliers
> 150 Brigade, 1/4th East Yorkshires, 1/4th and 1/5th Green Howards, 1/5th Durhams

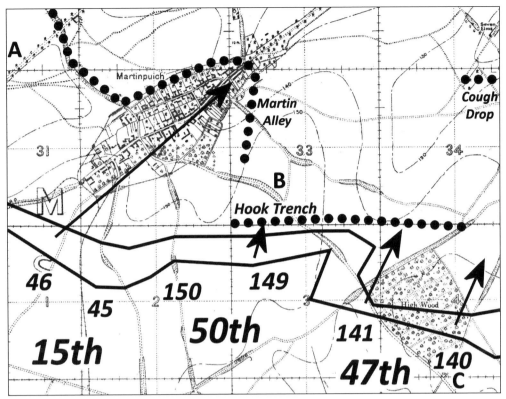

15 September, III Corps: 15th Division was able to capture Martinpuich but 50th Division's advance was compromised by 47th Division's failure to clear High Wood.

151 Brigade, 1/6th, 1/8th and 1/9th Durhams, 1/5th Borders
Pioneers, 1/7th Durhams: Artillery, CCL, CCLI, CCLII and CCLIII
   Brigades

47th (2nd London) Division, High Wood

Viewpoint C: 47th (2nd London) Division memorial, 100 metres west of the south corner of High Wood

The 1/18th, 1/17th, 1/20th and 1/19th London advanced through the west side of High Wood but their two tanks ditched. The 1/15th London were cut down at the east side of High Wood and the 1/7th London were stopped by Crest Trench; only a few crossed the Switch Line. A third tank ditched east of the wood while a fourth one mistook the 1/6th London for Germans and fired on them. The 1/8th London advanced to Flag Lane and the 1/6th London captured the Cough Drop.

The Londoners eventually cleared High Wood. At 6pm the 1/24th London failed to reached the Starfish Line but the 1/21st London reached Starfish Redoubt.

47th (2nd London) Division, Major General Charles Barter
140 Brigade, 1/6th, 1/7th, 1/8th and 1/15th London
141 Brigade, 1/17th, 1/18th, 1/19th and 1/20th London
142 Brigade, 1/21st, 1/22nd, 1/23rd and 1/24th London
Pioneers, 1/4th Welsh Fusiliers: Artillery, CCXXXV, CCXXXVI,
    CCXXXVII and CCXXXVIII Brigades

Memorial C: The 47th (London) Division memorial is 100 metres west of the south corner of High Wood.

Receiving instructions before zero hour.

15 September, XV Corps' Left

New Zealand Division, Flers
Viewpoint A: New Zealand memorial

The 2nd Otago Battalion overran Crest Trench under fire from High Wood as the 1st Auckland Battalion overran Coffee Lane and the Switch Line. Sergeant Donald Brown silenced two machine guns as the Otagos chased the Germans to the Switch Line; he was awarded the Victoria Cross.

The tanks trailed the 4th New Zealand Rifles advancing to Flag Lane and Fat Trench. The 3rd New Zealand Rifles waited two hours for them and, while one tank was disabled crossing Fat Trench, three crushed the wire and allowed the Rifles to reach Flers Trench. The 2nd New Zealand Rifles then captured Flers Support. The 1st New Zealand Rifles cleared Abbey Road and headed for Grove Alley with one tank. A counter-attack forced them to withdraw but the tank stopped on the Ligny road, near Box and Cox trenches.

New Zealand Division, Major General Sir Andrew Russell
1 Brigade, 1st Auckland, 1st Canterbury, 1st Otago, 1st Wellington
2 Brigade, 2nd Auckland, 2nd Canterbury, 2nd Otago, 2nd Wellington
3 Brigade, 1st, 2nd, 3rd and 4th New Zealand Rifle Brigade
Pioneers, New Zealand Pioneers: Artillery, 1st, 2nd, 3rd and 4th New Zealand Brigades

Memorial A: The New Zealand memorial is at the centre of the division's advance on 15 September; the memorial to the missing is in Caterpillar Valley Cemetery, Longueval.

41st Division, Flers
Viewpoint B: Junction on the Flers road, north side of Delville Wood
Viewpoint C: Hard-standing on road north of Flers

Three tanks helped the 18th KRRC and 15th Hampshires capture Tea Support and Flers Trench but they were all later disabled. Four tanks helped the 21st KRRC and 10th Queen's capture Tea Support and the Switch Line before leading the 26th and 32nd Royal Fusiliers to Flers Trench. One crawled through Flers accompanied by cheering infantry, while three cleared strongpoints east of the village.

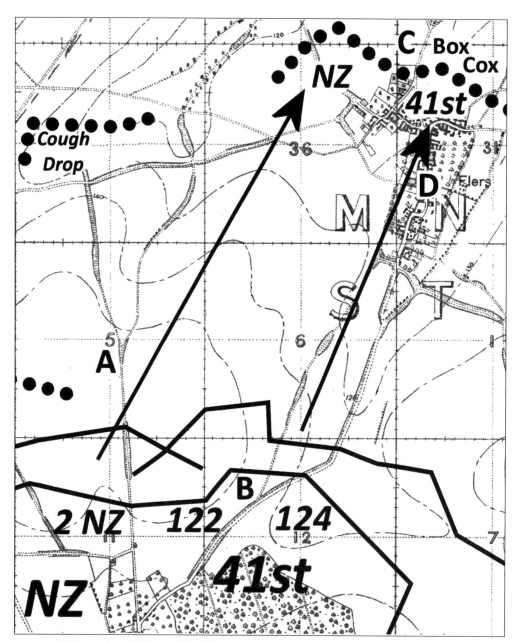

15 September, XV Corps Left: The New Zealand Division and 41st Division advanced alongside the tanks to Flers but the advance was compromised due to failures on the flanks.

The 18th KRRC, 8th East Surreys and 11th Queen's Own cleared Flers but rallied in Flers Trench, south of the village, because it was being shelled. Three tanks joined them around Box, Cox and the Hog's Head, north of Flers, at 3pm, but one returned to refuel, one was knocked out with the New Zealanders and one drove into 14th Division's sector. The only reinforcement was part of the 23rd Middlesex, which deployed along Bulls Road, east of Flers.

41st Division, Major General Sydney Lawford

122 Brigade, 12th East Surreys, 15th Hampshires, 11th Queen's Own, 18th KRRC

123 Brigade, 11th Queen's, 10th Queen's Own, 23rd Middlesex, 20th Durhams

124 Brigade, 10th Queen's, 26th and 32nd Royal Fusiliers, 21st KRRC

Pioneers, 19th Middlesex: Artillery, CLXXXIII (Howitzer), CLXXXVII, CLXXXIX and CXC Brigades

Memorial D: The 41st Division memorial stands in the centre of Flers.

Soldiers wait by a bogged down tank.

15 September, XV Corps' Right and XIV Corps' Left

14th (Light) Division, Gueudecourt
Viewpoint A: South-east corner of Delville Wood
Viewpoint B: Tree 200 m east of Bulls Road Cemetery

A tank advanced with the 6th KOYLI at 5.15am but it was disabled crossing Hop Alley; Ale Alley and Hop Alley were soon cleared. A tank helped the 8th KRRC and 8th Rifle Brigade overrun Tea Support and Pint Trench before it was disabled. They then captured the Switch Line as the 7th KRRC and 7th Rifle Brigade seized Gap Trench. The 5th Shropshires and 9th Rifle Brigade could not reach Bulls Road. The 5th Ox and Bucks and the 9th KRRC were stopped by Gird Trench. A tank made a lone crusade towards Gueudecourt before it was knocked out.

> 14th (Light) Division, Major General Victor Couper
> 41 Brigade, 7th KRRC, 8th KRRC, 7th Rifle Brigade, 8th Rifle Brigade
> 42 Brigade, 5th Ox & Bucks, 5th Shropshires, 9th KRRC, 9th Rifle Brigade
> 43 Brigade, 6th Somersets, 6th DCLI, 6th KOYLIs, 10th Durhams
> Pioneers, 11th King's: Artillery, XLVI, XLVII, XLVIII and XLIX Brigades

Guards Division, Lesboeufs
Viewpoint C: French memorial by Ginchy cemetery, north of the village
Viewpoint D: The Guards Division memorial, the Triangle

None of the ten allocated tanks reached the front line. The 3rd and 2nd Coldstream Guards advanced 'as steadily as though they were walking down the Mall'. The 1st Irish Guards mingled with the Coldstream after the 1st Coldstream Guards drifted into their path and they captured the wrong trench in the mist. The 2nd Grenadier Guards captured Serpentine Trench as the Coldstream Guards advanced to the sound of Lieutenant Colonel John Campbell's hunting horn. He 'led his men everywhere like a tiger' and would be awarded the Victoria Cross.

The 1st Coldstream Guards and 3rd Grenadier Guards veered left,

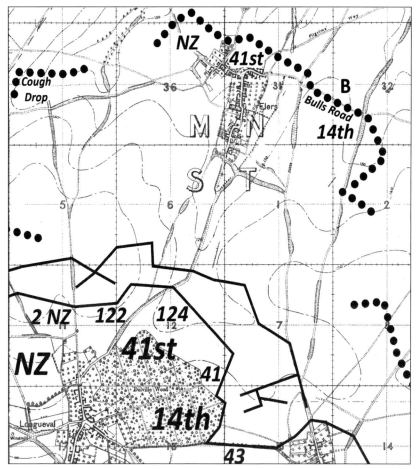

15 September, XV Corps Right and XIV Corps Left: 14th Division advanced to Flers as the Guards Division drifted north towards Serpentine Trench.

became mixed with the 2nd Irish Guards and 1st Scots Guards, and captured Serpentine Trench and the Triangle. A badly injured Lance Sergeant Frederick McNess stopped a counter-attack against the 1st Scots Guards' flank; he was awarded the Victoria Cross.

The 1st Welsh Guards and 1st Grenadiers struggled to assemble on 16 September and advanced late at 1.30pm, without artillery support. They were soon pinned down with their left on Punch Trench.

Guards Division, Major General Geoffrey Feilding
1 Brigade: 2nd Grenadier Guards, 2nd and 3rd Coldstream Guards,
   1st Irish Guards
2 Brigade: 3rd Grenadier Guards, 1st Coldstream Guards, 1st Scots
   Guards, 2nd Irish Guards
3 Brigade: 1st Grenadier Guards, 4th Grenadier Guards, 2nd Scots
   Guards, 1st Welsh Guards
Pioneers, 4th Coldstream Guards: Artillery, LXI, LXXIV, LXXV
   and LXXVI Brigades

*Memorial D: The Guards Division memorial stands next to the site of
Triangle strongpoint.*

An armoured car passes a Guards Division dressing station.

15 September, XIV Corps' Right

6th Division, The Quadrilateral
Viewpoint A: The Quadrilateral

The only working tank fired on the 9th Norfolks by mistake before heading north to Straight Trench rather than the Quadrilateral. The 1st Leicesters and 9th Norfolks were stopped by wire in front of Straight Trench and the tank then withdrew. The 8th Bedfords and 1st Buffs were pinned down by the Quadrilateral's machine guns.

A second attempt at 8.20am by the 1st Sherwoods and 9th Suffolks failed to take Straight Trench or the Quadrilateral. The 2nd Durhams cleared the wrong trench and the 11th Essex lost direction during a third attempt at 7.30pm.

6th Division, Major General Charles Ross
16 Brigade, 1st Buffs, 8th Bedfords, 1st Shropshires, 2nd York and Lancasters
18 Brigade, 1st West Yorkshires, 11th Essex, 2nd Durhams, 14th Durhams
71 Brigade, 9th Norfolks, 9th Suffolks, 1st Leicesters, 2nd Sherwoods
Pioneers, 11th Leicesters: Artillery, II, XXIV, XXXVIII Brigades

56th (1st London) Division, Bouleaux Wood
Viewpoint B: The Dickens memorial, overlooking Bouleaux Wood and Leuze Wood
Viewpoint C: The east side of Leuze Wood, overlooking Combles

A tank helped the 1/1st London reach Beef Trench before ditching. At 8.20am the 1/7th Middlesex failed to reach the north end of Bouleaux Wood. A tank was disabled near the Loop but the 1/2nd London bombed along Loop Trench and Combles Trench with the 1/5th London bombers. The 1/8th Middlesex advanced alone at 1.40pm because 6th Division had cancelled its attack and the Quadrilateral's machine guns halted them. Another attempt to take the Quadrilateral at 11pm also failed.

56th (1st London) Division, Major General Charles Hull
167 Brigade, 1/1st London, 1/3rd London, 1/7th and 1/8th Middlesex
168 Brigade, 1/4th, 1/12th, 1/13th and 1/14th London

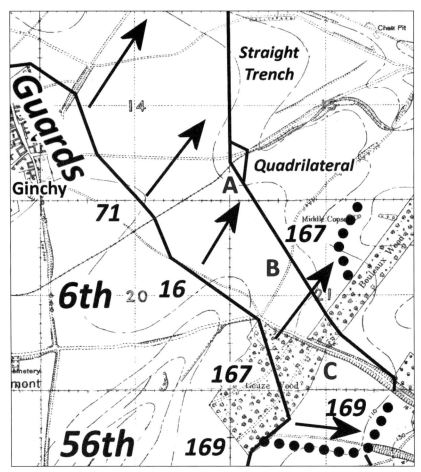

15 September, XIV Corps: 6th Division failed to capture the Quadrilateral but 56th Division made progress north and east of Leuze Wood.

169 Brigade, 1/2nd, 1/5th, 1/9th and 1/16th London
Pioneers, 1/5th Cheshires: Artillery, CCLXXX, CCLXXXI,
   CCLXXXII and CCLXXXIII Brigades

Assessment of the Tank

Thirty-six tanks had started out but less than a dozen had played a part because the rest broke down, ditched or were knocked out. Combined arms tactics had not been practiced because the tanks had been kept under a cloak of secrecy until the last moment. The Germans had panicked at the sight of them but they had not fled en masse. Lieutenant General Julian Byng of the Canadian Corps thought 'tanks are a useful accessory to the infantry, but nothing more'; however they had given his troops 'a feeling of superiority and security'. But 15 September was 'a very valuable try out' for the tanks and improved models would soon be delivered to the front.

16 to 22 September, III Corps

23rd Division, Martinpuich
Viewpoint A: Pull-in at the east end of Martinpuich

On 17 September 69 Brigade advanced from Crescent Alley and extended its hold on the Starfish Line and Prue Trench.

> 23rd Division, Major General James Babington
> 68 Brigade, 10th and 11th Northumberland Fusiliers, 12th and 13th Durhams
> 69 Brigade, 11th West Yorkshires, 8th Green Howards, 9th Green Howards, 10th Duke's
> 70 Brigade, 11th Sherwoods, 8th KOYLIs, 8th York and Lancasters, 9th York and Lancasters
> Pioneers, 9th South Staffords: Artillery, CII, CIII and CIV Brigades

50th (Northumbrian) Division, Starfish Line and Prue Trench
Viewpoint B: Hook Trench, west of High Wood

At 9.25am on 16 September the 1/5th Durhams failed to capture the west end of Prue Trench and Martin Alley. The 1/5th Borders and 1/9th Durhams captured the east end of Prue Trench for a time but had to withdraw. At 4.30pm on 18 September the 1/8th Durhams' bombers could not clear Crescent Trench but the 1/5th Durhams' bombers captured parts of the Starfish Line and Prue Trench.

> 50th (Northumbrian) Division, Major General Percival Wilkinson
> 149 Brigade, 1/4th, 1/5th, 1/6th and 1/7th Northumberland Fusiliers
> 150 Brigade, 1/4th East Yorkshires, 1/4th and 1/5th Green Howards, 1/5th Durhams
> 151 Brigade, 1/6th, 1/8th and 1/9th Durhams, 1/5th Borders
> Pioneers, 1/7th Durhams: Artillery, CCL, CCLI, CCLII and CCLIII Brigades

47th (2nd London) Division, Starfish Line and Flers Trench
Viewpoint B: Hook Trench, west of High Wood

The 1/23rd London advanced from Crest Trench at 8.55am on 16 September but most went no further than the Starfish Line. At 5am on 18 September

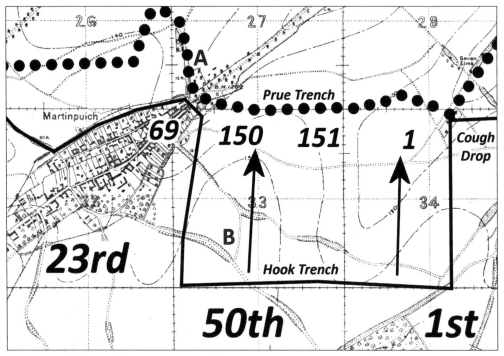

16 to 22 September, III Corps: While 23rd Division secured Martinpuich, 50th Division and 1st Division occupied an abandoned Prue Trench.

the 1/8th and 1/15th London captured Drop Alley and Flers Trench where they were reinforced by the 1/23rd and 1/24th London. By dusk on 19 September the 1/15th London had been driven from Drop Alley and Flers Trench, back to the Cough Drop. The Germans abandoned the Starfish Line and Prue Trench late on 21 September and they were occupied.

47th (2nd London) Division, Major General Charles Barter
140 Brigade, 1/6th, 1/7th, 1/8th and 1/15th London
141 Brigade, 1/17th, 1/18th, 1/19th and 1/20th London
142 Brigade, 1/21st, 1/22nd, 1/23rd and 1/24th London
Pioneers, 1/4th Welsh Fusiliers: Artillery, CCXXXV, CCXXXVI, CCXXXVII and CCXXXVIII Brigades

1st Division, North of High Wood
Viewpoint B: Hook Trench, west of High Wood
At 8.30pm on 20 September the 1st Black Watch advanced without a barrage and took the Flers Trenches and the Cough Drop by surprise. The following evening the abandoned Prue Trench was occupied.

1st Division, Major General Peter Strickland
1 Brigade, 10th Gloucesters, 1st Black Watch, 8th Berkshires, 1st Camerons
2 Brigade, 2nd Sussex, 1st Loyals, 1st Northants, 2nd KRRC
3 Brigade, 1st South Wales Borderers, 1st Gloucesters, 2nd Welsh, 2nd Munsters
Pioneers, 1/6th Welsh: Artillery, XXV, XXVI and XXXIX Brigades

A working party carries wiring material to the front.

16 to 22 September, XV Corps

New Zealand Division, Flers Trenches
Viewpoint A: Road west from Flers, past the water tower to the end of the road

At 9.25am on 16 September a tank helped the 1st Wellington Battalion advance towards Grove Alley until it was disabled. They then formed a flank as the 1st Canterbury Battalion dug back to Box and Cox. The 2nd Auckland Battalion and the 1st Otago Battalion bombers cleared Flers Support as far as Goose Alley on 18 September. The 2nd Canterbury Battalion captured the Flers Trenches and Goose Alley by surprise at 8.30pm on 20 September and then stopped a counter-attack.

New Zealand Division, Major General Sir Andrew Russell
1 Brigade, 1st Auckland, 1st Canterbury, 1st Otago, 1st Wellington Battalions
2 Brigade, 2nd Auckland, 2nd Canterbury, 2nd Otago, 2nd Wellington Battalions
3 Brigade, 1st, 2nd, 3rd and 4th New Zealand Rifle Brigade
Pioneers, New Zealand Pioneers: Artillery, 1st, 2nd, 3rd and 4th New Zealand Brigades

21st Division, Flers
Viewpoint B: Hard-standing on road north of Flers

On 16 September the 15th Durhams and 9th KOYLIs got lost in the rain and dark and advanced late, 1,300 metres short of their jumping off line. They were pinned down in front of Gird Trench while their tank was knocked out in front of Gueudecourt; the two battalions rallied on Bulls Road. The following morning the Germans bombed down Gas Alley.

21st Division, Major General David Campbell
62 Brigade, 12th and 13th Northumberland Fusiliers, 1st Lincolns, 10th Green Howards
64 Brigade, 9th KOYLIs, 10th KOYLIs, 14th Durhams, 15th Durhams
110 Brigade, 6th, 7th, 8th and 9th Leicesters.
Pioneers, 14th Northumberland Fusiliers: Artillery, XCIV, XCV and XCVI Brigades

14th (Light) Division, Gird Trenches
Viewpoint C: The single tree, 200 metres east of Bulls Road Cemetery

The creeping barrage started too far ahead of the infantry at 9.25am on 16 September, so the 10th Durhams were hit by machine gun fire in the Gird Trenches while the 6th Somersets were shot at from Gas Alley. The 6th DCLIs and the 6th KOYLIs went forward only to be pinned down. Many survivors were holding a trench incorrectly reported as Gird Trench. Another attempt to advance at 6.55pm also failed.

    14th (Light) Division, Major General Victor Couper
    41 Brigade, 7th KRRC, 8th KRRC, 7th Rifle Brigade, 8th Rifle
       Brigade
    42 Brigade, 5th Ox & Bucks, 5th Shropshires, 9th KRRC, 9th Rifle
       Brigade
    43 Brigade, 6th Somersets, 6th DCLIs, 6th KOYLIs, 10th Durhams
    Pioneers, 11th King's: Artillery, XLVI, XLVII, XLVIII and XLIX
       Brigades

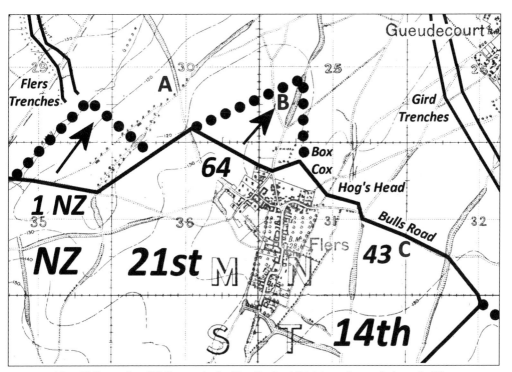

16 to 22 September, XV Corps: As the New Zealand Division advanced along the Flers Trenches and 21st pushed north of Flers village, 14th Division held its position.

16 to 22 September, XIV Corps

20th (Light) Division, Lesboeufs
Viewpoint A: Guards Division memorial, the Triangle

Orders were issued late to the 7th Somersets and 7th DCLIs of 20th Division and they eventually advanced towards their objective at 9.25am on 16 September. The delay to the Guards left them exposed, so the 12th King's covered their left flank while the 7th KOYLIs covered the right flank.

The Germans drove the 12th KRRC back when they attacked around 1.30pm on 17 September but the 6th Shropshires held their ground. The 11th KRRC, and the 10th and 11th Rifle Brigades then made a hurried advance north of the Lesboeufs road in the rain. Some troops did not get their orders in time, and the artillery had no time to time to plan their barrage. The battalions were shot at from all directions and soon halted when they advanced at 6.30pm because there were no other attacks in the area.

> 20th (Light) Division, Major General William Douglas-Smith
> 59 Brigade, 10th KRRC, 11th KRRC, 10th and 11th Rifle Brigade
> 60 Brigade, 6th Ox & Bucks, 6th Shropshires, 12th KRRC, 12th Rifle Brigade
> 61 Brigade, 7th Somersets, 7th DCLIs, 7th KOYLIs, 12th King's
> Pioneers, 11th Durhams: Artillery, XCI, XCII and XCIII Brigades

6th Division, Straight Trench and the Quadrilateral
Viewpoint B: The Quadrilateral

At 5.50am on 18 September the 1st West Yorkshires failed to reach Straight Trench in a direct attack but their bombers cleared 600 metres of trench. The 1st Shropshires overran the Quadrilateral from the north-east as the 14th Durhams cleared the dugouts along the Morval road on the left and the 2nd York and Lancasters moved up on the right.

> 6th Division, Major General Charles Ross
> 16 Brigade, 1st Buffs, 8th Bedfords, 1st Shropshires, 2nd York and Lancasters
> 18 Brigade, 1st West Yorkshires, 11th Essex, 2nd Durhams, 14th Durhams
> 71 Brigade, 9th Norfolks, 9th Suffolks, 1st Leicesters, 2nd Sherwoods

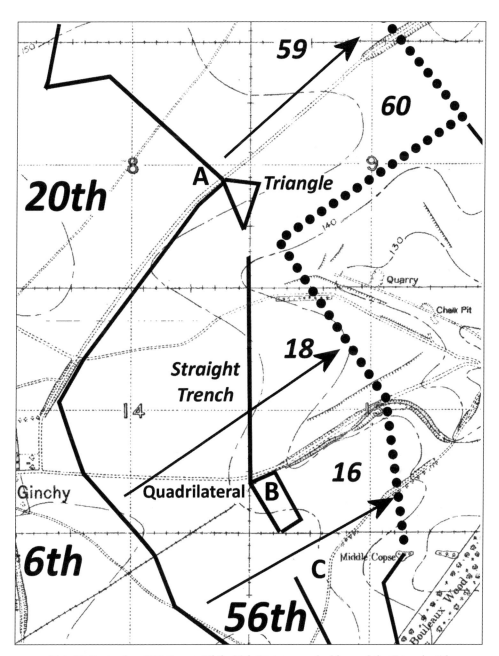

16 to 22 September, XIV Corps: While 20th Division pushed beyond the Triangle, 6th Division eventually captured Straight Trench and the Quadrilateral.

Pioneers, 11th Leicesters: Artillery, II, XXIV and XXXVIII
Brigades

56th (1st London) Division, Bouleaux Wood
Viewpoint C: The Dickens Memorial

On 16 September, mud delayed the 1/4th and 1/14th London Regiment and
they only just advanced on time; they were both stopped by machine gun
fire from Bouleaux Wood. The 1/16th and 1/2nd London Regiment were
pinned down approaching the sunken Combles road; but the 1/5th London
Regiment bombed towards the road. Few men returned across the wasteland
of shell-holes.

56th (1st London) Division, Major General Charles Hull
167 Brigade, 1/1st and 1/3rd London Regiment, 1/7th and 1/8th
Middlesex
168 Brigade, 1/4th, 1/12th, 1/13th and 1/14th London Regiment
169 Brigade, 1/2nd, 1/5th, 1/9th and 1/16th London Regiment
Pioneers, 1/5th Cheshires: Artillery, CCLXXX, CCLXXXI,
CCLXXXII and CCLXXXIII Howitzer Brigades

A howitzer crew waits under their camouflage for instructions.

25 to 29 September, III Corps

23rd Division, Twenty-Sixth Avenue
Viewpoint A: Leave north-east end of Martinpuich, just beyond village sign, pull-in on the right

At dawn on 24 September the Germans counter-attacked the 12th Durhams, east of the Bapaume road. The following day one tank ditched while the second was hit by artillery fire and withdrew. At 12.35pm on 25 September, the 10th Northumberland Fusiliers were halted by a hail of bullets advancing over the crest and the bombers could not clear Twenty-Sixth Avenue. On 27 September Major Shaw, an artillery observer, discovered Twenty-Sixth Avenue was abandoned, so it was occupied. At dawn on 29 September the 8th York and Lancaster captured Destremont Farm in pouring rain.

> 23rd Division, Major General James Babington
> 68 Brigade, 10th North'd Fusiliers, 11th North'd Fusiliers, 12th Durhams, 13th Durhams
> 69 Brigade, 11th West Yorkshires, 8th Green Howards, 9th Green Howards, 10th Duke's
> 70 Brigade, 11th Sherwoods, 8th KOYLIs, 8th York and Lancasters, 9th York and Lancasters
> Pioneers, 9th South Staffords: Artillery, CII, CIII and CIV Brigades

50th (Northumbrian) Division, Crescent Alley
Viewpoint B: Hook Trench hard-standing, west of High Wood

As 150 Brigade had captured its objective the night before, the 1/5th Durhams established an outpost in Crescent Alley. At 11pm on 26 September the 5th and 4th Green Howards captured Flers Switch and Crescent Alley without artillery support. The 1/5th Durhams cleared Twenty-Sixth Avenue and Crescent Alley at midday the following day.

> 50th (Northumbrian) Division, Major General Percival Wilkinson
> 149 Brigade, 1/4th, 1/5th, 1/6th and 1/7th Northumberland Fusiliers
> 150 Brigade, 1/4th East Yorkshires, 1/4th and 1/5th Green Howards, 1/5th Durhams
> 151 Brigade, 1/6th, 1/8th and 1/9th Durhams, 1/5th Borders
> Pioneers, 1/7th Durhams: Artillery, CCL, CCLI, CCLII and CCLIII Brigades

1st Division, Flers Trenches
Viewpoint B: Hook Trench hard-standing, west of High Wood

At 8.30pm on 24 September the 1st Black Watch failed to bomb along the Flers Trenches. They were successful the following day. At 11pm on 26 September 2 Brigade crept forward without artillery support but they lost their way in the dark. At noon the following day troops advanced towards the Flers Switch but they could not clear Flers Trench.

    1st Division, Major General Peter Strickland
    1 Brigade, 10th Gloucesters, 1st Black Watch, 8th Berkshires, 1st
      Camerons
    2 Brigade, 2nd Sussex, 1st Loyals, 1st Northants, 2nd KRRC
    3 Brigade, 1st South Wales Borderers, 1st Gloucesters, 2nd Welsh,
      2nd Munsters
    Pioneers, 1/6th Welsh: Artillery, XXV, XXVI and XXXIX Brigades

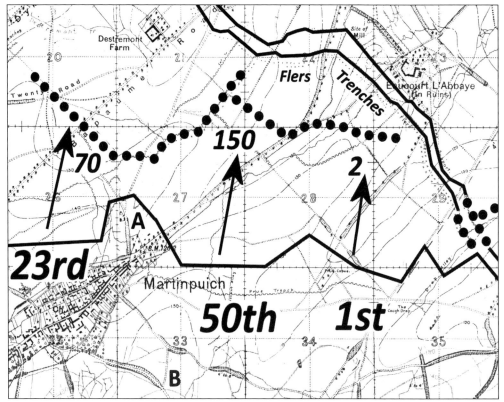

25 and 28 September, III Corps: 23rd and 50th Divisions advanced north of Martinpuich as 1st Division moved towards Eaucourt l'Abbaye.

25 to 26 September, XV Corps

New Zealand Division, North of Flers
Viewpoint A: Pull-in on crest west of Factory corner

At 12.35pm on 25 September the 1st Otago, 1st Auckland and 1st Canterbury Battalions encountered a few Germans advancing past Factory Corner. The Otagos then seized the south-west end of Goose Alley. At 2.15pm on 27 September the 1st Otagos were pinned down in front of Goose Alley. Meanwhile, the 1st Auckland and 1st Canterbury Battalions secured their parts of the Gird Trenches.

> New Zealand Division, Major General Sir Andrew Russell
> 1 Brigade, 1st Auckland, 1st Canterbury, 1st Otago, 1st Wellington Battalions
> 2 Brigade, 2nd Auckland, 2nd Canterbury, 2nd Otago, 2nd Wellington Battalions
> 3 Brigade, 1st, 2nd, 3rd and 4th New Zealand Rifle Brigade
> Pioneers, New Zealand Pioneers: Artillery, 1st, 2nd, 3rd and 4th Brigades

55th (West Lancashire) Division, the Gird Trenches
Viewpoint B: AIF Burial Ground

At 12.35pm on 25 September the 1/9th, 1/6th and 1/7th King's advanced to the Gird Trenches. The 1/9th King's then cleared Grove Alley while the 1/6th and 1/7th King's wheeled their right flank forward to the sunken road heading into Gueudecourt. At 2.15pm on 27 September the 1/8th King's overran the section of Gird Trenches north-west of Gueudecourt.

> 55th (West Lancashire) Division, Major General Hugh Jeudwine
> 164 Brigade, 1/4th King's Own, 1/4th Loyals, 1/8th King's, 2/5th Lancashire Fusiliers
> 165 Brigade, 1/5th, 1/6th, 1/7th and 1/9th King's
> 166 Brigade, 1/5th King's Own, 1/10th King's, 1/5th South Lancashires, 1/5th Loyals
> Pioneers, 1/4th South Lancashires: Artillery, CCLXXV, CCLXXVI, CCLXXVII and CCLXXVIII Brigades

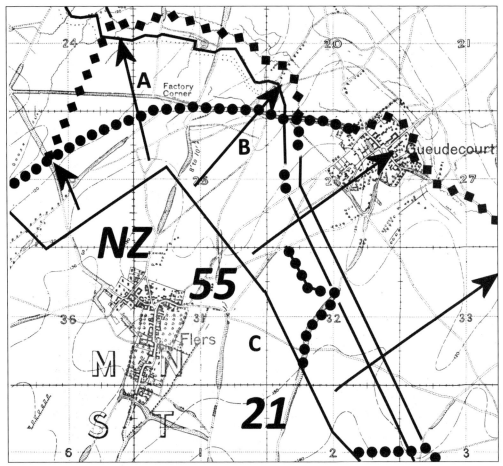

25 and 28 September, XV Corps: The New Zealand Division and 55th Division advanced north of Flers, but 21st Division could not clear the Gird Trenches covering Gueudecourt until the 26th.

21st Division, Gueudecourt

Viewpoint C: Tree 200 m east of Bulls Road Cemetery, Gird Trenches

At 12.35pm on 25 September the 8th and 9th Leicesters overran Goat Trench but machine gun fire stopped them reaching Gird Trench. A runner was wounded so the reserve companies did not move forward. The 8th Leicesters eventually reached Gird Trench but those who entered Gueudecourt were not seen again. The 1st East Yorkshires and 10th

KOYLIs were pinned down in front of Gird Trench but the 1st Lincolns advanced 'as if on parade without in any way having their morale shaken'.

On 26 September an aeroplane fired flares telling the artillery when to start and stop shelling Gird Trench. The plane strafed Gird Trench before a tank helped the 7th Leicesters clear it; the 15th Durhams followed up. The 19th Lancers and South Irish Horse reconnoitred Gueudecourt and the 6th Leicesters occupied the village during the late afternoon. The 15th Durhams and then the 12th Northumberland Fusiliers continued the advance; they were later joined by the 10th Green Howards.

21st Division, Major General David Campbell
62 Brigade, 12th and 13th Northumberland Fusiliers, 1st Lincolns, 10th Green Howards
64 Brigade, 9th and 10th KOYLIs, 14th and 15th Durhams
110 Brigade, 6th, 7th, 8th and 9th Leicesters
Pioneers, 14th Northumberland Fusiliers: Artillery, XCIV, XCV and XCVI Brigades

Transport waits to take men to the rear after an attack.

25 September, XIV Corps' Left Flank

Guards Division, North of Lesboeufs
Viewpoint A: Guards Cemetery

The 4th Grenadier Guards struggled to clear a new trench and lost the benefit of the barrage. They were unable to capture the junction of Gas Alley and Gird Trench, so they formed a defensive flank. The 2nd Scots Guards and the 1st Irish Guards encountered little resistance but the 2nd Grenadiers had to cut through three belts of wire to reach their objective.

During the final stage of the advance the Welsh Guards covered the open left flank as the 1st Grenadier Guards advanced north of Lesboeufs. The 2nd Grenadier Guards and the 1st Irish Guards cleared the north half of Lesboeufs.

Guards Division, Major General Geoffrey Feilding
1 Brigade: 2nd Grenadier Guards, 2nd and 3rd Coldstream Guards, 1st Irish Guards
2 Brigade: 3rd Grenadier Guards, 1st Coldstream Guards, 1st Scots Guards, 2nd Irish Guards

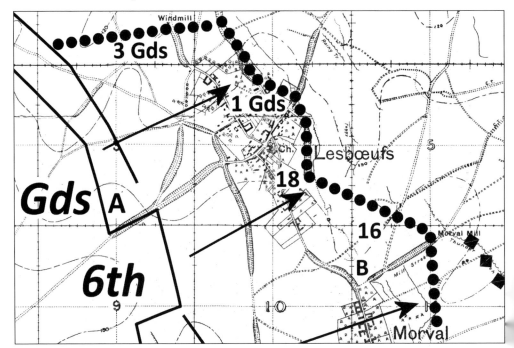

25 to 28 September, XIV Corps Left: The Guards Division and 6th Division worked together to clear Lesboeufs.

3 Brigade: 1st and 4th Grenadier Guards, 2nd Scots Guards, 1st Welsh Guards

Pioneers, 4th Coldstream Guards: Artillery, LXI, LXXIV, LXXV and LXXVI Brigades

6th Division, Lesboeufs

Viewpoint B: The crucifix at the north end of Morval

The 1st Buffs, 11th Essex and 2nd Durhams encountered little resistance and the 1st West Yorkshires cleared the south half of Lesboeufs. The 2nd York and Lancasters and the 1st Shropshires made a 'parade like, steady advance', east of the Lesboeufs–Morval road.

6th Division, Major General Charles Ross

16 Brigade, 1st Buffs, 8th Bedfords, 1st Shropshires, 2nd York and Lancasters

18 Brigade, 1st West Yorkshires, 11th Essex, 2nd Durhams, 14th Durhams

71 Brigade, 9th Norfolks, 9th Suffolks, 1st Leicesters, 2nd Sherwoods

Pioneers, 11th Leicesters: Artillery, II, XXIV, XXXVIII Brigades

Moving forward to consolidate the captured position.

25 September, XIV Corps' Right Flank

5th Division, Morval
Viewpoint A: The shrine on the Ginchy road, west of Morval

The 1st Norfolks occupied an empty trench because the garrison had withdrawn to shell holes to avoid the barrage. The 1st Bedfords and 1st Cheshires then moved to Morval before the 16th Warwicks advanced beyond the village. Private Thomas Jones of the Cheshires single-handedly captured over 100 Germans sheltering in dugouts; he was awarded the Victoria Cross.

The 1st Devons side-stepped north into 6th Division's sector to avoid a belt of wire. They then cleared the Bovril section of Gird Trench as the 1st East Surreys captured the Lemco section. The Devons, 1st Bedfords and East Surreys then advanced to a sunken road. An hour later the 1st Cheshires began clearing dugouts in the north end of Morval while the 2nd KOSBs and 12th Gloucesters did the same in the south half. The German artillery started firing at Morval so the 16th Warwicks moved 200 metres beyond the village at 6pm, as the 2nd York and Lancasters dug in between Lesboeufs and Morval mill.

> 5th Division, Major General Reginald Stephens
> 13 Brigade, 14th Warwicks, 15th Warwicks, 2nd KOSBs, 1st
>   Queen's Own
> 15 Brigade, 16th Warwicks, 1st Norfolks, 1st Bedfords, 1st
>   Cheshires
> 95 Brigade, 1st Devons, 12th Gloucesters, 1st East Surreys, 1st
>   DCLIs
> Pioneers, 1/6th Argylls: Artillery, XV, XVII and XVIII Brigades

56th (1st London) Division, Bouleaux Wood and Combles
Viewpoint B: The Dickens memorial
Viewpoint C: Hard-standing on the east side of Leuze Wood

Before dawn on 24 September the 1/9th London failed to make contact with the French in Combles Trench. At 12.28pm on the 25th the 1/14th London overran the trench north of Bouleaux Wood and another trench with views over Combles. There were rumours Combles was going to be evacuated and a detachment of the 1/14th London approached its north side during the night as the 1/4th London and 1/1st London checked an empty Bouleaux Wood.

At 2.10am red rockets followed by a green rocket was the signal for the Germans to abandon Combles and the 1/2nd London soon met French troops in the centre. The 1/5th London met them in Combles Trench and the 1/14th London contacted them on the north-east side of the village. It allowed 56th Division's north flank to move forward 1,000 metres and it dug in between Morval and Combles.

56th Division, Major General Charles Hull
167 Brigade, 1/1st London, 1/3rd London, 1/7th and 1/8th Middlesex
168 Brigade, 1/4th, 1/12th, 1/13th and 1/14th London
169 Brigade, 1/2nd, 1/5th, 1/9th and 1/16th London
Pioneers, 1/5th Cheshires: Artillery, CCLXXX, CCLXXXI, CCLXXXII and CCLXXXIII Howitzer Brigades

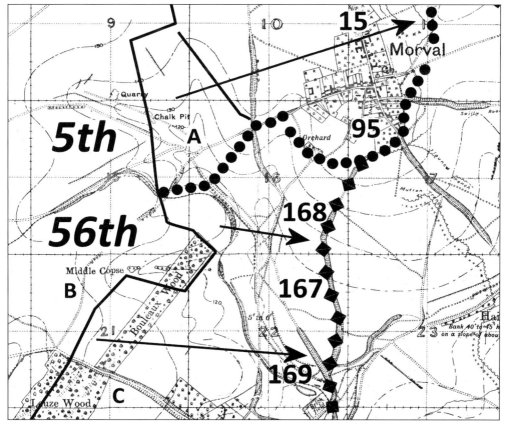

25 to 28 September, XIV Corps Right: 5th Division cleared Morval and 56th Division pushed east of Bouleaux Wood as the Germans withdrew from Combles.

25 September, II Corps

18th (Eastern) Division, Thiepval
Viewpoint A: Thiepval visitors centre

Zero hour was 12.35pm but the 11th Royal Fusiliers were delayed clearing Brawn Trench, south-west of Thiepval, and they lost the benefit of the barrage. The 12th Middlesex advanced into Thiepval, followed by two Fusilier companies and a tank, which soon ditched. During the Middlesex advance, Private Frederick Edwards silenced a machine gun, and Private Robert Ryder single-handedly cleared a trench; both Edwards and Ryder were awarded the Victoria Cross. The 6th Northants captured the chateau following a second barrage while the Fusiliers mopped up in the village.

The 8th Suffolks overran Joseph Trench but their accompanying tank ditched in Schwaben Trench. The 10th Essex cleared the sunken road running through Thiepval and the 8th Norfolks mopped up .The Suffolks and the Essex cleared Zollern Trench but could not reach Midway Trench.

18th (Eastern) Division, Major General Ivor Maxse
53 Brigade, 8th Norfolks, 8th Suffolks, 10th Essex, 6th Berkshires
54 Brigade, 11th Royal Fusiliers, 7th Bedfords, 8th Northants, 12th Middlesex
55 Brigade, 7th Queen's, 7th Buffs, 8th East Surreys, 7th Queen's Own
Pioneers, 8th Sussex: Artillery, LXXXII, LXXXIII, LXXXIV and LXXXV Brigades

Memorial B: 18th Division's memorial is opposite the exit the Thiepval visitor's centre car park.

11th (Northern) Division, Zollern and Stuff Redoubts, Mouquet Farm
Viewpoint C: Mouquet Farm, AIF memorial

The 6th Borders cleared Joseph Trench, Schwartz Trench, Zollern Trench and the Midway Line as the 7th South Staffords mopped up. The 9th Sherwoods could only capture the west end of Hessian Trench because Zollern Redoubt covered the east end.

The 9th Lancashire Fusiliers' bombers captured the Mouquet Farm garrison before zero hour, and the rest of the battalion crossed High Trench, heading for Zollern Redoubt. The 8th Northumberland Fusiliers also crossed High Trench.

Two tanks ditched early on, leaving the Lancashire Fusiliers, Northumberland Fusiliers and 5th Dorsets pinned down by Zollern Redoubt. The 11th Manchesters, 5th Dorsets and 6th East Yorkshires then cleared Mouquet Farm but it was impossible to take Zollern Redoubt.

11th (Northern) Division, Lieutenant General Sir Charles Woollcombe

32 Brigade, 9th West Yorkshires, 6th Green Howards, 8th Duke's, 6th York & Lancasters

33 Brigade, 6th Lincolns, 6th Borders, 7th South Staffords, 9th Sherwoods

34 Brigade, 8th North'd Fusiliers, 9th Lancashire Fusiliers, 5th Dorsets, 11th Manchesters

Pioneers, 6th East Yorkshires: Artillery, LVIII, LIX and LX Brigades

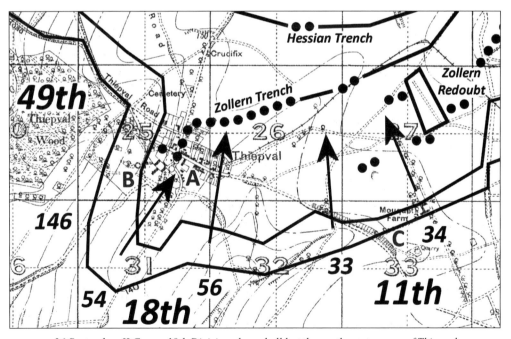

26 September, II Corps: 18th Division cleared all but the north-west corner of Thiepval village; but 11th Division struggled to reach Zollern Trench.

26 September, Canadian Corps

1st Canadian Division, Regina Trench
Viewpoint A: Regina Trench road, gravel crossroads on the crest

Machine guns fired overhead at 12:34pm on 26 September and a minute later the barrage began. Fire from Zollern and Stuff Redoubts pinned down Major McLeod's company on 8th Canadian Battalion's left flank but the rest overran Zollern and Hessian Trenches with 5th Canadian Battalion while the 10th Battalion mopped up. The 8th Battalion eventually had to evacuate Hessian Trench and 7th Canadian Battalion connected Zollern and Hessian Trenches.

The 15th Canadian Battalion moved between Zollern Trench and Sudbury Trench towards Regina Trench but had to withdraw under fire from Kenora Trench. The 14th Canadian Battalion cleared Sudbury Trench and the east end of Kenora Trench. It drove off counter-attacks with 16th Canadian Battalion's help.

  1st Canadian Division, Major General Arthur Currie
  1 Brigade, 1st, 2nd, 3rd and 4th Canadian Battalions
  2 Brigade, 5th, 7th, 8th and 10th Canadian Battalions
  3 Brigade, 13th, 14th, 15th and 16th Canadian Battalions
  Pioneers, 1st Canadian Pioneer Battalion: Artillery, 1st, 2nd and 3rd
    Canadian Brigades

2nd Canadian Division, Courcelette
Viewpoint B: Courcelette civilian cemetery

The 4th Canadian Battalion stopped the Germans entering the north-east corner of Courcelette on the night of 17/18 September and then occupied trenches east of the village.

Machine guns fired overhead at 12.34pm on 26 September and a minute later the barrage began. The 31st Canadian Battalion was stopped by crossfire from Sudbury Trench but 29th Canadian Battalion captured its objective. The two tanks detailed to clear the trenches east of Courcelette were soon out of action while artillery fire stopped 28th Battalion leaving their trenches. At 10.50pm 31st and 27th Canadian Battalions captured Sudbury Trench.

2nd Canadian Division, Major General Richard Turner
4 Brigade, 18th, 19th, 20th and 21st Canadian Battalions
5 Brigade, 22nd, 24th, 25th and 26th Canadian Battalions
6 Brigade, 27th, 28th, 29th and 31st Canadian Battalions
Pioneers, 2nd Canadian Pioneer Battalion: Artillery, 4th, 5th, 6th
    and 7th Brigades

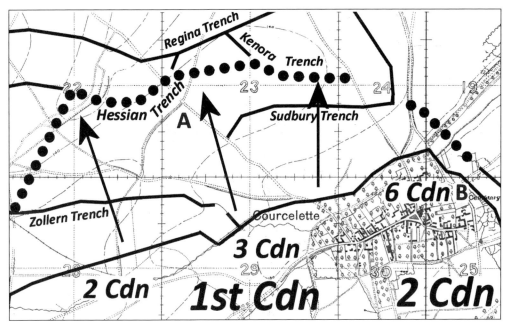

*26 September, Canadian Corps: While 1st Canadian Division captured Hessian Trench,
2nd Canadian Division improved its position east of Courcelette.*

25 to 30 September, II Corps

18th (Eastern) Division, Thiepval
Viewpoint A: Thiepval civilian cemetery

At 5.45am on 27 September, the 7th Bedfords advanced before the barrage ended, encouraged by an injured Second Lieutenant Tom Adlam, and they captured the north-west corner of Thiepval. At the same time the 10th Essex bombers cleared Bulgar Trench.

At 1pm on 28 September the 7th Bedfords cleared the trenches parallel to Mill Road, as the 7th Queen's and the 8th Suffolks captured Bulgar Trench and Martin Trench. They then seized Midway Trench, heading for the east end of the redoubt. Second Lieutenant Adlam, despite his wounds, inspired the 7th Bedfords to take the trenches facing Thiepval Wood; he was awarded the Victoria Cross.

A counter-attack at dawn on 30 September drove the 7th Queen's Own and 8th East Surreys from Schwaben Redoubt. The Queen's Own and 7th Buffs failed to retake the west face but the East Surreys recaptured the south and north side; they were driven from the north face back to Stuff Trench during the evening.

> 18th (Eastern) Division, Major General Ivor Maxse
> 53 Brigade, 8th Norfolks, 8th Suffolks, 10th Essex, 6th Berkshires
> 54 Brigade, 11th Royal Fusiliers, 7th Bedfords, 8th Northants, 12th Middlesex
> 55 Brigade, 7th Queen's, 7th Buffs, 8th East Surreys, 7th Queen's Own
> Pioneers, 8th Sussex: Artillery, LXXXII, LXXXIII, LXXXIV and LXXXV Brigades

11th (Northern) Division, Zollern and Hessian Trenches
Viewpoint B: Stump Road Cemetery

At 10am on 27 September the 9th Lancashire Fusiliers were engaged in Zollern Trench, the 8th Northumberland Fusiliers fought for Zollern Redoubt and 11th Manchesters reached Zollern Trench. The 6th Borders reinforced the 7th South Staffords and 9th Sherwood Foresters. The Borders cleared Hessian Trench and the Staffords cleared Zollern Trench. Zero hour on 26 September was delayed but the 9th West Yorkshires advanced alone to Stuff Redoubt at 3pm. There was no barrage when the 6th Green Howards advanced an hour later and they took Hessian Trench by surprise.

The Stuff Redoubt fighting continued until the 6th York and Lancasters cleared it and part of Hessian Trench on 29 September; the 7th South Staffords helped hold it. At 4pm on 30 September the 7th South Staffords and 6th York and Lancasters secured Stuff Redoubt. Captain Archie White of the 6th Green Howards was awarded the Victoria Cross for his leadership during the fighting.

   11th (Northern) Division, Lieutenant General Sir Charles Woollcombe
   32 Brigade, 9th West Yorkshires, 6th Green Howards, 8th Duke's, 6th York & Lancasters
   33 Brigade, 6th Lincolns, 6th Borders, 7th South Staffords, 9th Sherwoods
   34 Brigade, 8th North'd Fusiliers, 9th Lancashire Fusiliers, 5th Dorsets, 11th Manchesters
   Pioneers, 6th East Yorkshires: Artillery, LVIII, LIX and LX Brigades

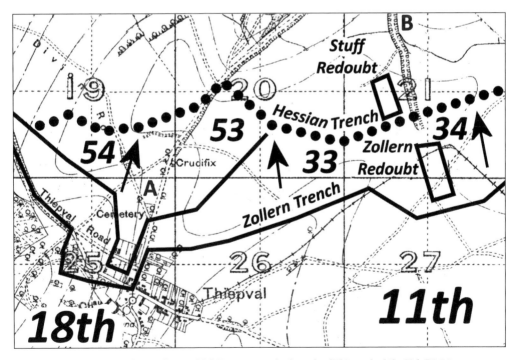

27 to 30 September, II Corps: 18th Division pushed north of Thiepval while 11th Division cleared Zollern Redoubt and captured Hessian Trench.

27 to 30 September, Canadian Corps

1st Canadian Division, Zollern and Hessian Trenches
Viewpoint A: Regina Trench road, gravel crossroads on the crest

The 7th Canadian Battalion spent 27 September clearing Hessian Trench but machine guns in Stuff Redoubt swept the area between Zollern and Hessian Trenches. Later that night patrols reported that Regina Trench was empty. The 14th Canadian Battalion continued to fight for Kenora Trench until it was exhausted. It made its last attempt at 2am on 28 September when the final seventy-five men still standing advanced; the Germans illuminated the area with flares and halted the attack, inflicting heavy casualties.

> 1st Canadian Division, Major General Arthur Currie
> 1 Brigade, 1st, 2nd, 3rd and 4th Canadian Battalions
> 2 Brigade, 5th, 7th, 8th and 10th Canadian Battalions
> 3 Brigade, 13th, 14th, 15th and 16th Canadian Battalions
> Pioneers, 1st Canadian Pioneer Battalion: Artillery, 1st, 2nd and 3rd
>   Canadian Brigades

3rd Canadian Division, Hessian Trench
Viewpoint A: Regina Trench road, gravel crossroads on the crest

The 2nd Canadian Mounted Rifles captured part of Hessian Trench on 29 and 30 September.

> 3rd Canadian Division, Major General Louis Lipsett
> 7 Brigade, Princess Patricia's, Royal Canadian Regiment, 42nd and
>   49th Canadian Battalions
> 8 Brigade, 1st, 2nd, 4th and 5th Canadian Mounted Rifles (CMRs)
> 9 Brigade, 43rd, 52nd, 58th and 60th Canadian Battalions
> Pioneers, 3rd Canadian Pioneer Battalion: Artillery, 8th, 9th, 10th
>   and 11th Artillery Brigades

2nd Canadian Division, Courcelette and Regina Trench
Viewpoint B: Adanac Cemetery
Viewpoint C: Courcelette civilian cemetery

Late on 27 September 31st and 28th Canadian Battalions saw the Germans withdrawing from the trenches facing Courcelette, so they occupied them. A cavalry patrol rode towards Le Sars at dawn to see how far the Germans had withdrawn; it came under fire from Destremont Farm and retired. At 7am 26th Canadian Battalion failed to advance far astride Courcelette Trench while 24th Canadian Battalion's attack on Regina Trench was stopped by wire. After reliefs, 21st Canadian Battalion made a little progress and 19th Canadian Battalion could not get any closer to Destremont Farm.

The 23rd Division captured Destremont Farm early on 29 September, so 19th and 21st Canadian Battalions moved up alongside. All the patrols which approached Regina Trench later that evening came under fire. Twenty-four hour postponement was then called for, following complaints that the Canadian artillery was shooting short.

2nd Canadian Division, Major General Richard Turner
4 Brigade, 18th, 19th, 20th and 21st Canadian Battalions
5 Brigade, 22nd, 24th, 25th and 26th Canadian Battalions
6 Brigade, 27th, 28th, 29th and 31st Canadian Battalions
Pioneers, 2nd Canadian Pioneer Battalion: Artillery, 4th, 5th, 6th
    and 7th Brigades

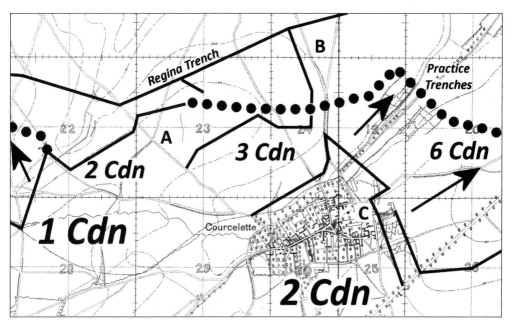

27 to 30 September, Canadian Corps: 1st and 2nd Canadian Divisions pushed north of Courcelette.

1 to 14 October, II Corps

18th (Eastern) Division, Schwaben Redoubt
Viewpoint A: Thiepval civilian cemetery

The fight for Schwaben Redoubt continued on 1 October and the trenches between the German front line and the east end of the redoubt were lost the following morning. Mud stopped the 8th Norfolks entering the redoubt on the morning of 5 October.

> 18th (Eastern) Division, Major General Ivor Maxse
> 53 Brigade, 8th Norfolks, 8th Suffolks, 10th Essex, 6th Berkshires
> 54 Brigade, 11th Royal Fusiliers, 7th Bedfords, 8th Northants, 12th Middlesex
> 55 Brigade, 7th Queen's, 7th Buffs, 8th East Surreys, 7th Queen's Own
> Pioneers, 8th Sussex: Artillery, LXXXII, LXXXIII, LXXXIV and LXXXV Brigades

39th Division, Schwaben Redoubt
Viewpoint A: Thiepval civilian cemetery

On 8 October the 17th and 16th Sherwoods stopped a flamethrower attack. Early on 9 October the 16th Sherwoods captured the north face of the redoubt but could not hold it because the trench was so deep in mud. At 2.45pm on 14 October the 1/6th Cheshires advanced along the German front line while the 4/5th Black Watch, the 1/1st Cambridge and the 17th KRRC cleared Schwaben Redoubt in a fight which lasted into the night. Counter-attacks with flamethrowers were stopped the following day.

> 39th Division, Major General Gerald Cuthbert
> 116 Brigade, 11th, 12th and 13th Sussex, 14th Hampshire
> 117 Brigade, 16th and 17th Sherwoods, 17th KRRC, 16th Rifle Brigade
> 118 Brigade, 1/6th Cheshires, 1/1st Cambridge, 1/1st Hertfords and 4/5th Black Watch
> Pioneers, 13th Gloucesters: Artillery, CLXXIV, CLXXIX, CLXXXIV and CLXXXVI Brigades

25th Division, Stuff Redoubt
Viewpoint B: Stump Road Cemetery

At 12.35pm on 9 October the 10th Cheshires advanced through the north
side of Stuff Redoubt. The Germans spent the next three days trying to
dislodge the Cheshires and the 8th Loyals, who relieved them. The Loyals
captured the Mounds, north-west of the redoubt, at 2.45pm on 14 October.

25th Division, Major General Guy Bainbridge
7 Brigade, 10th Cheshires, 3rd Worcesters, 8th Loyals, 1st
   Wiltshires
74 Brigade, 11th Lancashire Fusiliers, 13th Cheshires, 9th Loyals,
   2nd Irish Rifles
75 Brigade, 11th Cheshires, 8th Borders, 2nd South Lancashires,
   8th South Lancashires
Pioneers, 6th South Wales Borderers: Artillery, CX, CXI, CXII and
   CXIII Brigades

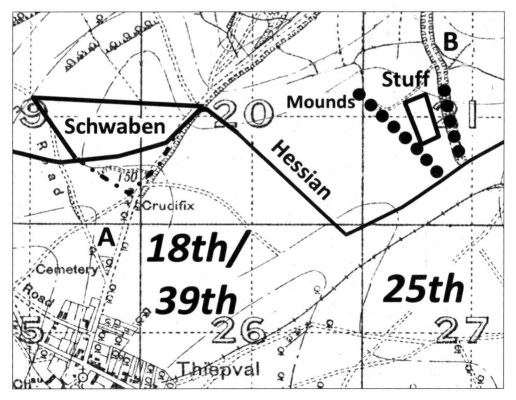

*1 to 14 October, II Corps: 18th and 39th Division faced a prolonged struggle on
Schwaben Redoubt as 25th Division fought for Stuff Redoubt.*

1 and 8 October, Canadian Corps

3rd Canadian Division, Regina Trench and North-West of Courcelette
Viewpoint A: Adanac Cemetery

The preliminary barrage either overshot or hit the 4th and 5th Canadian Mounted Rifles on 1 October. They then struggled through the mud at 3.15pm only to be stopped. Only two groups entered Regina Trench and while one was overwhelmed the other withdrew.

At 4.50am on 8 October the 49th Canadian Battalion's left reached Regina Trench while the right entered the north end of Kenora Trench and became casualties. Parts of the Royal Canadian Regiment, and 43rd and 58th Canadian Battalions trudged through the mud in pouring rain to Regina Trench, but their footholds in the position were easily contained and they were forced to withdraw before they could be surrounded.

> 3rd Canadian Division, Major General Louis Lipsett
> 7 Brigade, Princess Patricia's, Royal Canadian Regiment, 42nd and 49th Canadian Battalion
> 8 Brigade, 1st, 2nd, 4th and 5th Canadian Mounted Rifles (CMRs)
> 9 Brigade, 43rd, 52nd, 58th and Canadian 60th Battalions
> Pioneers, 3rd Canadian Pioneer Battalion: Artillery, 8th, 9th, 10th and 11th Canadian Brigades

2nd Canadian Division, Regina Trench
Viewpoint A: Adanac Cemetery

On 1 October two parties of 24th Canadian Battalion reached Regina Trench but one was wiped out while the other blocked the north end of Kenora Trench. Although 25th Canadian Battalion reached Kenora Trench, only a handful reached the wire protecting Regina Trench. A few of 22nd Canadian Battalion also reached Regina Trench but they were overwhelmed. Machine gun fire stopped 18th and 20th Canadian Battalions in front of Regina Trench, north of Courcelette.

> 2nd Canadian Division, Major General Richard Turner
> 4 Brigade, 18th, 19th, 20th and 21st Canadian Battalions
> 5 Brigade, 22nd, 24th, 25th and 26th Canadian Battalions
> 6 Brigade, 27th, 28th, 29th and 31st Canadian Battalions

Pioneers, 2nd Canadian Pioneer Battalion: Artillery, 4th, 5th, 6th
and 7th Canadian Brigades

1st Canadian Division, North-East of Courcelette
Viewpoint B: Practice Trenches lane, north-east of Courcelette

On 8 October Piper Jimmy Richardson played his pipes until the 13th and
16th Canadian Battalions cut through the wire. The 3rd and 4th Canadian
Battalions followed through the gap in the wire and the four battalions
cleared the Quadrilateral and part of the Le Sars Line between them. One
by one the groups withdrew and Piper Richardson was escorting prisoners
to the rear when he remembered he had left his pipes behind. He returned
to look for them and was never seen again; Richardson was posthumously
awarded the Victoria Cross.

    1st Canadian Division, Major General Arthur Currie
    1 Brigade, 1st, 2nd, 3rd and 4th Canadian Battalions
    2 Brigade, 5th, 7th, 8th and 10th Canadian Battalions
    3 Brigade, 13th, 14th, 15th and 16th Canadian Battalions
    Pioneers, 1st Canadian Pioneer Battalion: Artillery, 1st, 2nd and 3rd
       Canadian Brigades

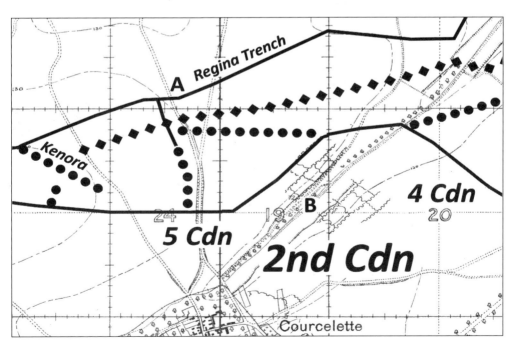

*1 to 8 October, Canadian Corps: 2nd Canadian Division captured Kenora Trench and
advanced towards Regina Trench.*

1 to 7 October, III Corps

23rd Division, Le Sars
Viewpoint A: Parking south-west of Destremont Farm
Viewpoint B: Quarry, north-west of Le Sars

At 3.15pm on 1 October the 8th KOYLIs and 9th York and Lancasters captured Flers Trench and the 11th Sherwoods then cleared Flers Support. At 6pm on 3 October the 10th Duke's failed to reach Flers Support and Second Lieutenant Henry Kelly returned, carrying his injured sergeant major. He later rescued three more men and would be awarded the Victoria Cross. The 11th Northumberland Fusiliers could not capture the Tangle on 6 October.

At 1.45pm on 7 October the 9th Green Howards, followed by the 12th and 13th Durhams, cleared Le Sars. North-west of Le Sars the 11th West Yorkshires' bombers started clearing Flers Support with the 10th Duke's. The 8th York and Lancasters captured the rest the following morning.

> 23rd Division, Major General James Babington
> 68 Brigade, 10th and 11th Northumberland Fusiliers, 12th and 13th Durhams
> 69 Brigade, 11th West Yorkshires, 8th Green Howards, 9th Green Howards, 10th Duke's
> 70 Brigade, 11th Sherwoods, 8th KOYLIs, 8th and 9th York and Lancasters
> Pioneers, 9th South Staffords: Artillery, CII, CIII and CIV Brigades

50th (Northumbrian) Division, South of Le Sars
Viewpoint C: Tangle pull-in, east of Le Sars

On 1 October the 1/5th Northumberland Fusiliers failed to reach Flers Trench but the 1/5th Borders and the 1/8th Durhams captured both Flers trenches. The 1/6th Durhams took Flers Trench and Lieutenant Colonel Roland Bradford of the 1/9th Durhams helped them clear Flers Support; he was awarded the Victoria Cross.

> 50th (Northumbrian) Division, Major General Percival Wilkinson
> 149 Brigade, 1/4th, 1/5th, 1/6th and 1/7th Northumberland Fusiliers

150 Brigade, 1/4th East Yorkshires, 1/4th and 1/5th Green Howards,
 1/5th Durhams
151 Brigade, 1/6th, 1/8th and 1/9th Durhams, 1/5th Borders
Pioneers, 1/7th Durhams: Artillery, CCL, CCLI, CCLII and CCLIII
 Brigades

47th (2nd London) Division, Eaucourt l'Abbaye
Viewpoint D: Entrance to Eaucourt l'Abbaye

At 3.15pm on 1 October the 1/17th London failed to take the Flers trenches
but two tanks helped the 1/20th and 1/19th London reach them before
ditching. The 1/23rd London could not capture the Flers trenches north of
Eaucourt l'Abbaye the following morning but the 1/18th London cleared
them on 3 and 4 October.

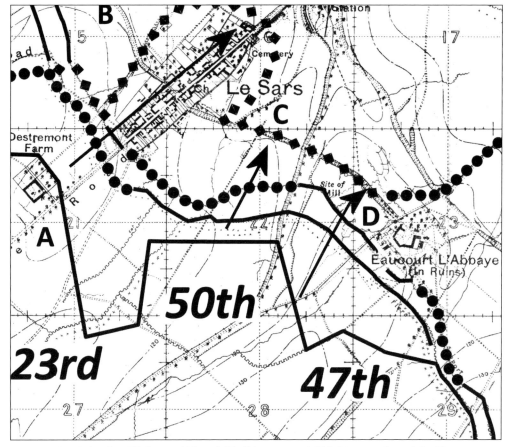

*1 to 7 October, III Corps: Although 23rd Division and 50th Division cleared the Flers
Trenches in front of Le Sars, 47th Division struggled to advance towards Eaucourt
l'Abbaye.*

On 7 October the 1/8th and 1/7th London and 1/15th London failed to clear the Nose and Snag Trench. Later that night the 1/22nd London captured part of Snag Trench but the 1/21st London could not take the adjacent trench.

47th (2nd London) Division, Major General Sir George Gorringe
140 Brigade, 1/6th, 1/7th, 1/8th and 1/15th London
141 Brigade, 1/17th, 1/18th, 1/19th and 1/20th London
142 Brigade, 1/21st, 1/22nd, 1/23rd and 1/24th London
Pioneers, 1/4th Welsh Fusiliers: Artillery, CCXXXV, CCXXXVI,
    CCXXXVII and CCXXXVIII Brigades

The Butte de Warlencourt memorial.

1 October, III and XV Corps

New Zealand Division, Goose Alley
Viewpoint A: Hard-standing east of Eaucourt l'Abbaye

At 3.15pm on 1 October, thirty Liven Projectors around Goose Alley fired burning oil over the Gird Trenches. Then the Otago Battalion advanced past the Circus and stopped on the Le Barque road, north-east of Eaucourt l'Abbaye. The Canterbury Battalion cleared the east end of Circus Trench and the German end of the Gird Trenches.

New Zealand Division, Major General Sir Andrew Russell
1 Brigade, 1st Auckland, 1st Canterbury, 1st Otago, 1st Wellington
2 Brigade, 2nd Auckland, 2nd Canterbury, 2nd Otago, 2nd
Wellington
3 Brigade, 1st, 2nd, 3rd and 4th New Zealand Rifle Brigade
Pioneers, New Zealand Pioneers: Artillery, 1st, 2nd, 3rd and 4th
Brigades

41st Division, Gird and Flers Trenches
Viewpoint B: Pull-in west of Factory Corner

On 7 October burning oil was sprayed across the Gird Trenches, but the barrage moved forward too quickly and machine gun fire stopped the 15th Hampshires. The 11th Queen's Own bombers could not clear the Flers Trenches and the 18th KRRC and 12th East Surreys stopped German counter-attacks. Machine guns stopped the 26th and 32nd Royal Fusiliers reaching Bayonet Trench and neither the 10th Queen's nor the 21st KRRC could help.

41st Division, Major General Sydney Lawford
122 Brigade, 12th East Surreys, 15th Hampshires, 11th Queen's
Own, 18th KRRC
123 Brigade, 11th Queen's, 10th Queen's Own, 23rd Middlesex,
20th Durhams
124 Brigade, 10th Queen's, 26th and 32nd Royal Fusiliers, 21st
KRRC
Pioneers, 19th Middlesex: Artillery, CLXXXIII, CLXXXVII,
CLXXXIX and CXC Brigades

12th (Eastern) Division, Hilt Trench and Bayonet Trench
Viewpoint C: AIF Cemetery

On 7 October artillery fire disorganised the 8th and 9th Royal Fusiliers before zero hour and they were then stopped by machine gun fire from Bayonet Trench. A few 6th Buffs reached Rainbow Trench and a few 6th Queen's Own entered Hilt Trench, but they withdrew at dusk.

> 12th (Eastern) Division, Major General Arthur Scott
> 35 Brigade, 7th Norfolks, 7th Suffolks, 9th Essex, 5th Berkshires
> 36 Brigade, 8th Royal Fusiliers, 9th Royal Fusiliers, 7th Sussex, 11th Middlesex
> 37 Brigade, 6th Queen's, 6th Buffs, 7th East Surreys, 6th Queen's Own
> Pioneers, 5th Northants: Artillery, LXII, LXIII and LXIV Brigades

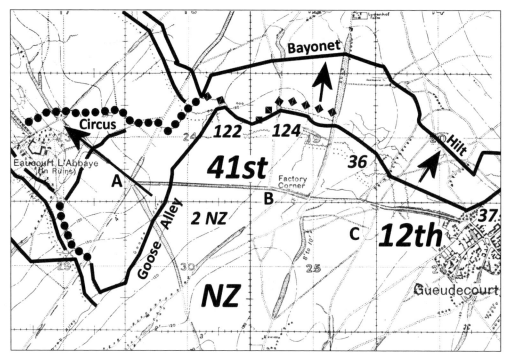

1 to 7 October, XV Corps: The New Zealand Division advanced past Eaucourt l'Abbaye but 41st Division struggled to get closer to Bayonet Trench and 12th Division could not capture Hilt Trench.

7 October, XIV Corps

The 6th Division and the Guards Division occupied abandoned trenches beyond Gueudecourt and Lesboeufs on 29 September; 20th Division did the same two days later.

20th (Light) Division, East of Gueudecourt
Viewpoint A: Road junction, north of Lesboeufs, Rainbow Trench

At 1.45pm on 7 October the Germans climbed out of Rainbow Trench to surrender to the 12th King's and 7th KOYLIs. The King's and the KOYLIs then dug a new trench beyond the obliterated Cloudy Trench. The 12th Rifle Brigade and 6th Ox & Bucks suffered heavy casualties cutting through the wire but they, too, were met by surrendering Germans, from Misty Trench.

> 20th (Light) Division, Major General William Douglas-Smith
> 59 Brigade, 10th KRRC, 11th KRRC, 10th Rifle Brigade, 11th Rifle Brigade
> 60 Brigade, 6th Ox & Bucks, 6th Shropshires, 12th KRRC, 12th Rifle Brigade
> 61 Brigade, 7th Somersets, 7th DCLI, 7th KOYLIs, 12th King's
> Pioneers, 11th Durhams: Artillery, XCI, XCII and XCIII Brigades

56th (1st London) Division, East of Lesboeufs
Viewpoint B: Lesboeufs civilian cemetery, Rainy Trench

The 1/7th Middlesex captured Rainbow Trench but the 1/1st London were pinned down in front of Spectrum Trench. The 1/14th London cleared a line of gun pits and the south end of Hazy Trench but the 1/4th London and 1/12th London were unable to reach Dewdrop Trench. The 1/4th London moved through the 1/14th London to take their objective but a counter-attack after dusk forced them to withdraw.

The following morning the troops withdrew from Spectrum Trench and Rainy Trench so the heavy artillery could shell the German trenches. The exhausted men struggled to get out of the muddy trenches at 3.30pm and machine gun fire stopped the 1/3rd London re-entering Spectrum Trench. The 1/9th London reached Dewdrop Trench and the 1/5th London captured Hazy Trench but they were both driven out during the night.

56th (1st London) Division, Major General Charles Hull
167 Brigade, 1/1st London, 1/3rd London, 1/7th and 1/8th
  Middlesex
168 Brigade, 1/4th, 1/12th, 1/13th and 1/14th London
169 Brigade, 1/2nd, 1/5th, 1/9th and 1/16th London
Pioneers, 1/5th Cheshires: Artillery, CCLXXX, CCLXXXI,
  CCLXXXII and CCLXXXIII Howitzer Brigades

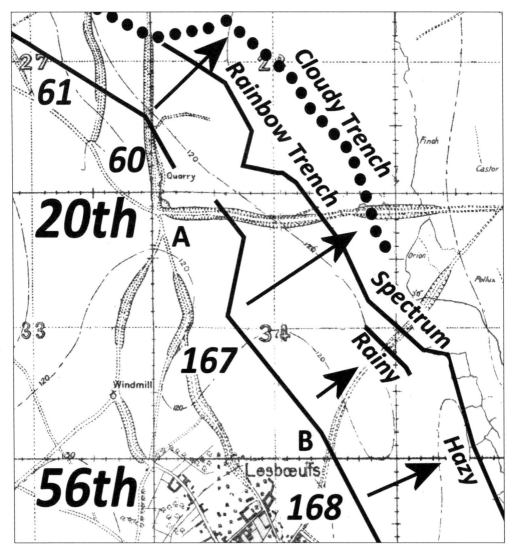

*1 to 7 October, XIV Corps: 20th Division captured Rainbow Trench and Cloudy Trench
but 56th Division could not take Rainy Trench or Spectrum Trench.*

12 to 18 October, III Corps

9th (Scottish) Division, Snag Trench
Viewpoint A: Quarry, west of Le Sars
Viewpoint B: The Tangle, east of Le Sars

The barrage and smoke screen were inaccurate, so the 2nd and 4th South African Regiments were halted when they advanced at 2.05pm on 12 October. Artillery fire and machine gun stopped the 7th Seaforths going far. The 10th Argylls failed to carry them forward. On the night of 14 October the 3rd South Africans captured the Pimple but they could not clear Snag Trench.

On 18 October 15th Division used tear gas and smoke to screen 9th Division's advance. At 3.40am the 1st South Africans and the 5th Camerons cleared more of Snag Trench in heavy rain. By nightfall the Germans had been pushed back to the Nose and the 8th Black Watch stopped a flamethrower attack the following morning.

At 4pm on 20 October the 6th KOSBs waded across a 'sea of pewter-grey ooze', firing a green flare every fifty metres so that the artillery lengthened their range. They eventually captured the Nose and part of Snag Trench. The 11th Royal Scots also cleared part of the Tail.

9th (Scottish) Division, Major General William Furse
26 Brigade, 8th Black Watch, 7th Seaforths, 5th Camerons, 10th Argylls
27 Brigade, 11th and 12th Royal Scots, 6th KOSBs, 9th Scottish Rifles
South African Brigade, 1st 2nd, 3rd and 4th South African Regiments
Pioneers, 9th Seaforths: Artillery, L, LI and LII Brigades

50th (Northumbrian) Division, Butte de Warlencourt and Hook Sap
Viewpoint C: Butte de Warlencourt

At 11.10am on 5 November, the 1/9th Durhams crossed Butte Trench and Butte Alley; some reached the summit of the Butte while others reached the Warlencourt Line on the Bapaume road. A few 1/6th Durhams reached the Butte but the rest were pinned down alongside the 1/8th Durhams. The Germans soon recaptured the Butte and Butte Trench.

Just before dawn on 14 November, the 1/7th Northumberland Fusiliers advanced towards Hook Sap; they never returned. The 1/4th and 1/5th Northumberland Fusiliers also failed to reach Hook Sap at midnight.

50th (Northumbrian) Division, Major General Percival Wilkinson
149 Brigade, 1/4th, 1/5th, 1/6th and 1/7th Northumberland Fusiliers
150 Brigade, 1/4th East Yorkshires, 1/4th and 1/5th Green Howards,
    1/5th Durhams
151 Brigade, 1/6th, 1/8th and 1/9th Durhams, 1/5th Borders
Pioneers, 1/7th Durhams: Artillery, CCL, CCLI, CCLII and CCLIII
    Brigades

Memorial C: Butte de Warlencourt is like a Romano-Gallic burial mound next to the Bapaume road, close to Warlencourt-Eaucourt. It represents the limit of the British advance in 1916. In 1990 the Western Front Association bought the Butte and erected a memorial on the summit.

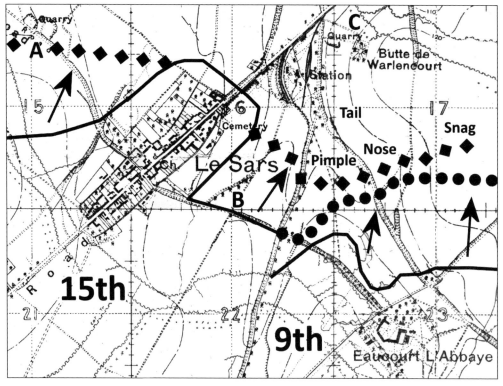

12-18 October, III Corps: 15th Division improved its position around Le Sars as 9th Division captured Snag Trench.

12 to 18 October, XV Corps

29th Division, Gird Trenches
Viewpoint A: Pull-in on crest west of Factory Corner

The 17th King's were silhouetted as they advanced down the slope at 2.05pm on 12 October and machine guns behind Gird Trench brought them to a halt. The 2nd Bedfords captured Bite Trench but they could not clear the Gird Trenches. Only a few of the 17th Manchesters reached Bayonet Trench while the 2nd Scots Fusiliers were stopped in no man's land.

    29th Division, Major General Henry de Beauvoir de Lisle
    86 Brigade, 2nd Royal Fusiliers, 1st Lancashire Fusiliers, 16th
        Middlesex, 1st Dublin Fusiliers
    87 Brigade, 2nd South Wales Borderers, 1st KOSBs, 1st
        Inniskilling Fusiliers, 1st Borders
    Pioneers, 2nd Monmouths: Artillery, XV, XVII and CXLVII
        Brigades

30th Division, Gird Trenches
Viewpoint B: Hard-standing on the left, north of Factory Corner
Viewpoint C: AIF Burial Ground

On 18 October two tanks failed to help the 2nd Wiltshires reach Snag Trench and the 18th King's reach the Nose in pouring rain; they both fell back. The 2nd Green Howards were pinned down in front of Rainbow Trench and Bite Trench. A tank reached Gird Trench the following morning but the infantry were too disorganised to occupy it and it withdrew.

    30th Division, Major General John Shea
    21 Brigade, 18th King's Own, 19th Manchesters, 2nd Green Howards,
        2nd Wiltshires
    89 Brigade, 17th King's, 19th King's, 20th King's, 2nd Bedfords
    90 Brigade, 16th Manchesters, 17th Manchesters, 18th Manchesters,
        2nd Scots Fusiliers
    Pioneers, 11th South Lancashires: Artillery, CXLVIII, CXLXIX and
        CL Brigades

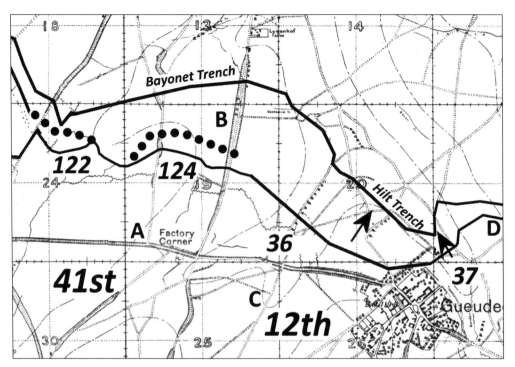

12 to 18 October, XV Corps: 41st Division inched towards Bayonet Trench but 12th Division could not clear Hilt Trench.

12th (Eastern) Division, Hilt Trench and Bayonet Trench
Viewpoint D: Newfoundland memorial, north of Gueudecourt

At 2.05pm on 12 October the 7th Norfolks and 7th Suffolks were stopped by the wire covering Bayonet Trench. The 1st Essex and the Newfoundland Regiment advanced north of Gueudecourt but had to retire to Hilt Trench. The 9th Essex were stopped by wire at 3.40am the following morning and the 1st Essex and 2nd Hampshires found that Grease Trench offered no cover. A few Hampshires reached Stormy Trench but they had to withdraw.

On 18 October the 9th Essex's left entered Bayonet Trench but had to withdraw because the right was held up by wire. The 4th Worcesters and 2nd Hampshires captured Grease Trench but could not advance further.

12th (Eastern) Division, Major General Arthur Scott
35 Brigade, 7th Norfolks, 7th Suffolks, 9th Essex, 5th Berkshires

36 Brigade, 8th Royal Fusiliers, 9th Royal Fusiliers, 7th Sussex, 11th Middlesex
37 Brigade, 6th Queen's, 6th Buffs, 7th East Surreys, 6th Queen's Own
Pioneers, 5th Northants: Artillery, LXII, LXIII and LXIV Brigades
Attached from 29th Division
88 Brigade, 4th Worcesters, 2nd Hampshires, 1st Essex, 1st Newfoundland Regiment

Memorial D: The Newfoundland Caribou memorial marks the limit of the advance in this area in 1916. The battalion did not get this far in the October attack.

The Newfoundland Caribou at Gueudecourt.

12 to 18 October, XIV Corps

6th Division, Rainbow, Cloudy and Mild Trenches
Viewpoint A: Road junction, north of Lesboeufs

The British barrage hit the 1st West Yorkshires before zero hour at 2.05pm on 12 October, stopping them reaching Cloudy Trench and Mild Trench. The 14th Durhams captured Rainbow Trench and then bombed back along the sunken road to cover the Yorkshires' exposed right flank. The 9th Suffolks held Cloudy Trench and Misty Trench while the 2nd York and Lancasters tried to capture Zenith Trench. The 11th Essex advanced beyond Mild Trench and bombed along the Beaulencourt road early on 15 October, but they were later forced back. Meanwhile, the 2nd Sherwoods captured gun pits east of Cloudy Trench.

On 18 October the 9th Norfolks lost the benefit of the barrage because of the deep mud, advancing from Shine Trench, and became disorientated in the darkness. A few entered Mild Trench but no one reached Cloudy Trench and many were taken prisoner.

> 6th Division, Major General Charles Ross
> 16 Brigade, 1st Buffs, 8th Bedfords, 1st Shropshires, 2nd York and Lancasters
> 18 Brigade, 1st West Yorkshires, 11th Essex, 2nd Durhams, 14th Durhams
> 71 Brigade, 9th Norfolks, 9th Suffolks, 1st Leicesters, 2nd Sherwoods
> Pioneers, 11th Leicesters: Artillery, II, XXIV, XXXVIII Brigades

4th Division, Spectrum, Zenith, Dewdrop and Rainy Trenches
Viewpoint B: Lesboeufs civilian cemetery
Machine guns hidden in no man's land stopped the 2nd Lancashire Fusiliers and the 2nd Duke's reaching Zenith Trench on 12 October. The 1st Irish Fusiliers were delayed by their barrage, allowing the Germans to man Dewdrop and Rainy Trenches. The Irish Fusiliers' right and the 1st Warwicks' left were stopped by a strongpoint; but the Warwicks' right reached Antelope Trench.

The 1st King's Own could not bomb along Spectrum Trench at 6.30pm on 14 October; a second attempt the following night also failed. The 2nd Dublin Fusiliers failed to take the gun pits in front of Hazy Trench. The 2nd

Seaforths captured Rainy Trench and the nearby gun pits but a counter-attack forced them to withdraw.

On 18 October there was a bombing fight for Spectrum Trench and the 1st King's Own cleared part of Dewdrop Trench. The 1st East Lancashires could not reach Rainy Trench or Dewdrop Trench while the 1st Rifle Brigade could not hold the gun pits near Hazy Trench. The 1st Somersets occupied an abandoned Frosty Trench the following evening.

4th Division, Major General the Hon William Lambton
10 Brigade, 1st Warwicks, 2nd Seaforths, 1st Irish Fusiliers, 2nd Dublin Fusiliers
11 Brigade, 1st Somersets, 1st East Lancashires, 1st Hampshires, 1st Rifle Brigade
12 Brigade, 1st King's Own, 2nd Lancashire Fusiliers, 2nd Essex, 2nd Duke's
Pioneers, 21st West Yorkshires: Artillery, XIV, XXIX and XXXII Brigades

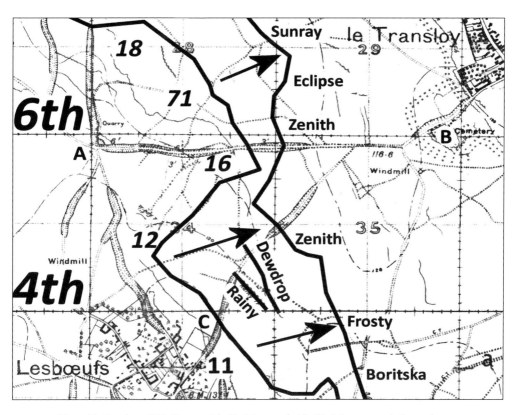

12 to 18 October, XIV Corps: 6th Division and 4th Division struggled to advance towards Le Transloy.

21 October, II Corps' Left

39th Division, Stuff Trench
Viewpoint A: North of Thiepval cemetery

The 14th Hampshires and 17th KRRC fought to stop Germans armed with flamethrowers capturing the north side of Schwaben Redoubt. At 12.06pm the 16th Rifle Brigade and 17th Sherwoods captured the Pope's Nose salient but the 14th Hampshires and 11th Sussex floundered in deep mud in Stuff Trench. Meanwhile, the 13th Sussex struggled to bomb along the old German Second Line.

> 39th Division, Major General Gerald Cuthbert
> 116 Brigade, 11th, 12th and 13th Sussex, 14th Hampshire
> 117 Brigade, 16th and 17th Sherwoods, 17th KRRC, 16th Rifle
>   Brigade

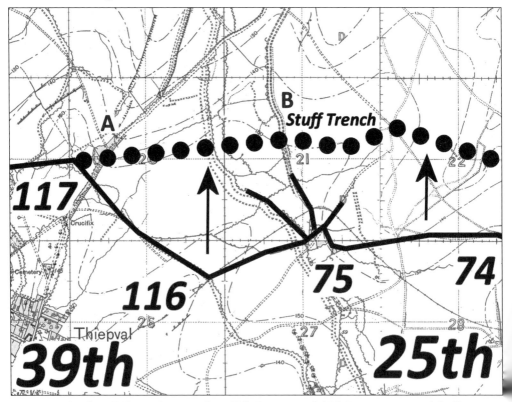

21 October, II Corps: Between them 39th Division and 25th Division captured Stuff Trench.

A Lewis gun crew provides covering fire.

118 Brigade, 1/6th Cheshires, 1/1st Cambridge, 1/1st Hertfords and 4/5th Black Watch

Pioneers, 13th Gloucesters: Artillery, CLXXIV, CLXXIX, CLXXXIV and CLXXXVI Brigades

25th Division, Stuff Trench
Viewpoint B: Stump Road Cemetery

The British barrage stopped the 2nd South Lancashires advancing west of the Pozières–Miraumont road. The 8th South Lancashire bombers cleared dugouts along Stump Road and the 8th Borders went beyond the objective to silence a gun battery. The 13th Cheshires, 9th Loyals and 11th Lancashire Fusiliers captured Stuff Trench.

25th Division, Major General Guy Bainbridge

7 Brigade, 10th Cheshires, 3rd Worcesters, 8th Loyals, 1st Wiltshires

74 Brigade, 11th Lancashire Fusiliers, 13th Cheshires, 9th Loyals, 2nd Irish Rifles

75 Brigade, 11th Cheshires, 8th Borders, 2nd South Lancashires, 8th South Lancashires

Pioneers, 6th South Wales Borderers: Artillery, CX, CXI, CXII and CXIII Brigades

21 October, II Corps' Right

18th (Eastern) Division, Stuff Trench
Viewpoint A: Regina Trench road, gravel crossroads on the crest

The 8th Norfolks won a bombing fight along the Grandcourt road. The 10th Essex occupied Regina Trench when the Germans eventually surrendered.

18th (Eastern) Division, Major General Ivor Maxse
53 Brigade, 8th Norfolks, 8th Suffolks, 10th Essex, 6th Berkshires
54 Brigade, 11th Royal Fusiliers, 7th Bedfords, 8th Northants, 12th
  Middlesex
55 Brigade, 7th Queen's, 7th Buffs, 8th East Surreys, 7th Queen's
  Own
Pioneers, 8th Sussex: Artillery, LXXXII, LXXXIII, LXXXIV and
  LXXXV Brigades

19th (Western) Division, Stuff Redoubt
Viewpoint A: Regina Trench road, gravel crossroads on the crest

Before dawn on 26 October the 7th East Lancashires stopped the Germans retaking Stuff Redoubt.

19th (Western) Division, Major General Tom Bridges
56 Brigade, 7th King's Own, 7th East Lancashires, 7th South
  Lancashires, 7th Loyals
57 Brigade, 10th Warwicks, 8th Gloucesters, 10th Worcesters, 8th
  North Staffords
58 Brigade, 9th Cheshires, 9th Welsh Fusiliers, 9th Welsh, 6th
  Wiltshires
Pioneers, 5th South Wales Borderers: Artillery, LXXXVI,
  LXXXVII and LXVIII Brigades

4th Canadian Division, Regina Trench
Viewpoint B: Adanac Cemetery

At 12.06pm the 102nd Canadian Battalion captured part of Regina Trench while the 87th Canadian Battalion formed a defensive flank, east of the Pys road. The 44th Canadian Battalion tried to extend its hold on Regina Trench at 7am on 25 October but the Canadian artillery failed to shell the Quadrilateral and machine gun fire stopped the attack.

4th Canadian Division, Major General David Watson
10 Brigade, 44th, 46th, 47th and 50th Canadian Battalions
11 Brigade, 54th, 75th, 87th and 102nd Canadian Battalions
12 Brigade, 38th, 72nd, 73rd and 78th Canadian Battalions
Pioneers, 67th Canadian (Pioneer) Battalion: Artillery, V, XI and
    XVIII Brigades (all British artillery)

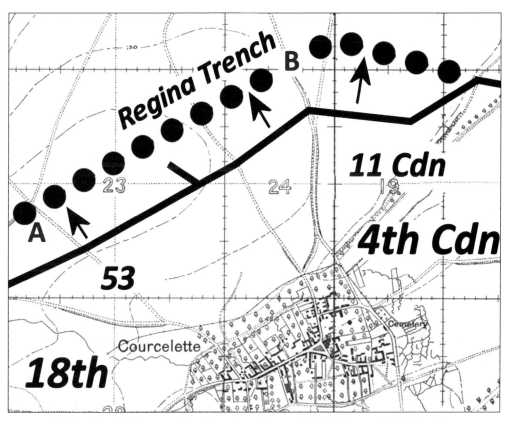

21 October, II Corps and the Canadian Corps: 18th Division and 4th Canadian Divisions worked together to clear Regina Trench.

23 October, XIV Corps

8th Division, Zenith Trench
Viewpoint A: Le Transloy cemetery

At 2.30pm the 2nd East Lancashires cleared Mild Trench but the 2nd Rifle Brigade could not capture the strongpoint at the junction of Eclipse and Zenith Trenches. The British barrage stopped the Germans escaping so they stood and fought in Zenith Trench, stopping the 2nd Lincolns crossing no man's land. The 2nd Middlesex and the 2nd Scottish Rifles stormed the south end of Zenith Trench and the Rifles held Orion Trench for a while. At 3.50am on 24 October the 1st Irish Rifles and 2nd Berkshire lost the benefit of the barrage because of the mud and were 'simply swept away'.

> 8th Division, Major General Havelock Hudson
> 23 Brigade, 2nd Devons, 2nd West Yorkshires, 2nd Middlesex, 2nd Scottish Rifles
> 24 Brigade, 1st Worcesters, 1st Sherwoods, 2nd Northants, 2nd East Lancashires
> 25 Brigade, 2nd Lincolns, 2nd Berkshires, 1st Irish Rifles, 2nd Rifle Brigade
> Pioneers, 22nd Durhams: Artillery, V (RHA), XXXIII and XLV Brigades

4th Division, Spectrum and Dewdrop Trenches
Viewpoint B: Lesboeufs civilian cemetery, Rainy Trench

The 1st King's Own advanced beyond Spectrum Trench and the 2nd Duke's bombers moved along the Le Transloy road but they later withdrew to Spectrum Trench. The 2nd Essex were hit by machine gun fire and the few men who reached Dewdrop Trench became casualties or were captured. The 2nd Dublin Fusiliers secured gun pits and a strongpoint but the advance was delayed when they became mixed up with the 1st Warwicks. A wounded Sergeant Downie repeatedly shouted 'Come on the Dubs' as they overran the trench beyond, but enfilade fire from Boritska Trench stopped them going further. Downie was later awarded the Victoria Cross. Boritska Trench's machine guns pinned down the 1st Hampshires while reinforcements from the 1st Rifle Brigade veered left to avoid the fire. They dug in alongside the Dublins.

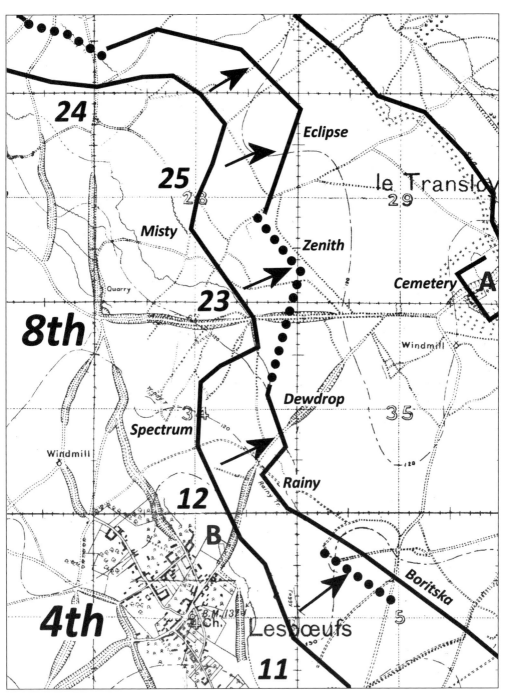

23 October, XIV Corps: Both 8th Division and 4th Division struggled to make progress towards Le Transloy because of the strongpoint in its cemetery.

4th Division, Major General the Hon William Lambton

10 Brigade, 1st Warwicks, 2nd Seaforths, 1st Irish Fusiliers, 2nd
   Dublin Fusiliers

11 Brigade, 1st Somersets, 1st East Lancashires, 1st Hampshires,
   1st Rifle Brigade

12 Brigade, 1st King's Own, 2nd Lancashire Fusiliers, 2nd Essex,
   2nd Duke's

Pioneers, 21st West Yorkshires: Artillery, XIV, XXIX and XXXII
   Brigades

Tired and dirty troops come out of the line.

28 October to 4 November, XIV Corps

17th (Northern) Division, Zenith and Eclipse Trenches
Viewpoint A: Le Transloy cemetery

At 5.30pm on 2 November the 7th Borders captured part of Zenith Trench and the 7th Lincolns cleared more the following day with the 7th Green Howards' bombers. Patrols from the 7th East Yorkshires and 7th Green Howards could not advance far from Zenith Trench on 5 November.

Major General Robertson GOC of 17th Division, summarised the terrible conditions: 'The weather conditions have been simply appalling and the trenches awful; men buried in mud, several deaths from exposure alone, men drowned in mud… I wonder if those behind the lines have the slightest conception of what it is like.'

> 17th (Northern) Division, Major General Philip Robertson
> 50 Brigade, 10th West Yorkshires, 7th East Yorkshires, 7th Green
>   Howards, 6th Dorsets
> 51 Brigade, 7th Lincolns, 7th Borders, 8th South Staffords, 10th
>   Sherwoods
> 52 Brigade, 9th North'd Fusiliers, 10th Lancashire Fusiliers, 9th
>   Duke's, 12th Manchesters
> Pioneers, 7th York and Lancasters: Artillery, LXXVIII, LXXIX
>   and LXXX Brigades

33rd Division, East of Lesboeufs
Viewpoint A: Le Transloy Cemetery
Viewpoint B: Lesboeufs civilian cemetery, Rainy Trench

The 4th King's and the 1st Middlesex cleared Dewdrop Trench and Rainy Trench at 6am on 28 October (the divisional history says it was the 2nd Worcesters and 1/4th Suffolks). At 5.45am the following morning the 5th/6th Scottish Rifles captured the north end of Boritska Trench but machine gun fire stopped the 1st Scottish Rifles; all the Scots withdrew later.

At 5.45am on 1 November some of the 5/6th Scottish Rifles reached Boritska Trench but the 1st Scottish Rifles were pinned down in no man's land. The 2nd Worcesters and the 1/9th Highland Light Infantry waited 'up

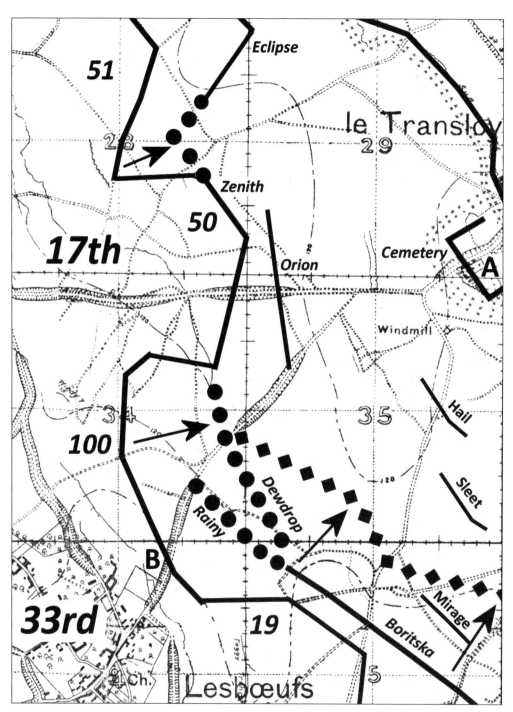

28 October, XIV Corps: While 17th Division could not get closer to Le Transloy, 33rd Division captured Rainy and Dewdrop Trenches.

to the waist in slime' for zero hour but at 3.30pm they could not reach Boritska Trench due to machine guns around Le Transloy cemetery.

At 4pm on 3 November the barrage supplied by French guns overshot the target, allowing the Germans to shoot the 1st Queen's down in front of Boritska Trench. The following day 98 Brigade could not reach the ridge east of Dewdrop trench.

At 12.30am on 5 November the Le Transloy cemetery machine guns pinned down the 2nd Welsh Fusiliers in pouring rain. But the 16th KRRC captured Hazy Trench as the 2nd Worcesters charged into Boritska Trench and Mirage Trench.

33rd Division, Major General Reginald Pinney
98 Brigade, 4th King's, 1/4th Suffolk, 1st Middlesex, 2nd Argylls
100 Brigade, 1st Queen's, 2nd Worcesters, 16th KRRC, 1/9th HLI
19 Brigade, 20th Royal Fusiliers, 2nd Welsh Fusiliers, 1st Scottish
    Rifles, 1/5th Scottish Rifles
Pioneers, 18th Middlesex: Artillery, CLVI, CLXII and CLXVI
    Brigades

Dragging a field gun through the mud.

5 to 18 November, I ANZAC Corps

2nd Australian Division, the Maze
Viewpoint A: Pull-in on crest west of Factory Corner

Some companies advanced at 12.30am on 5 November in pouring rain, only for their barrage to land behind them. Some companies moved out three minutes late and they could not keep up with the barrage in the mud. While 28th Australian Battalion was pinned down in front of the Gird trenches, a composite battalion captured the Maze in the centre and 27th Battalion entered Bayonet Trench. They held the isolated positions all day, but abandoned them after nightfall.

On 18 November, 19th Australian Battalion reached Gird Support only to find it flooded, so they withdrew to Gird Trench. Both 25th and 26th Australian Battalions were stopped by machine gun fire as they advanced towards the Maze. A later attack against the Maze also failed.

2nd Australian Division, Major General James Legge
5 (New South Wales) Brigade, 17th, 18th, 19th and 20th Battalions
6 (Victoria) Brigade, 21st, 22nd, 23rd and 24th Battalions
7 Brigade, 25th, 26th, 27th and 28th Battalions
Pioneers, 2nd Australian Pioneer Battalion: Artillery, 4th, 5th and
    6th Australian Brigades

1st Australian Division, Hilt Trench
Viewpoint B: Hard-standing on the left, north of Factory Corner
Viewpoint C: AIF Burial Ground

The 1st Battalion lost the benefit of the barrage in the mud and could not take Hilt Trench. The 3rd Battalion's bombers entered Lard Trench and advanced along Hilt Trench. Others joined a bombing group moving up the Le Thilloy road. They all withdrew when their bombs ran out.

1st Australian Division, Major General Harold Walker
1 (New South Wales) Brigade, 1st, 2nd, 3rd and 4th Battalions
2 (Victoria) Brigade, 5th, 6th, 7th and 8th Battalions
3 Brigade, 9th, 10th, 11th and 12th Battalions
Pioneers, 1st Australian Pioneer Battalion: Artillery, 1st, 2nd and
    3rd Australian Brigades

The Australians on the Somme

Over 28,000 Australians were killed or wounded on the Somme, the majority in the fighting around Pozières in July and August. The Australian missing are remembered on the memorial in Villers-Bretonneux Cemetery, site of Australian actions in April and August 1918. The New Zealand missing of the 1916 Somme battle are commemorated on the memorial in Caterpillar Valley Cemetery, Longueval.

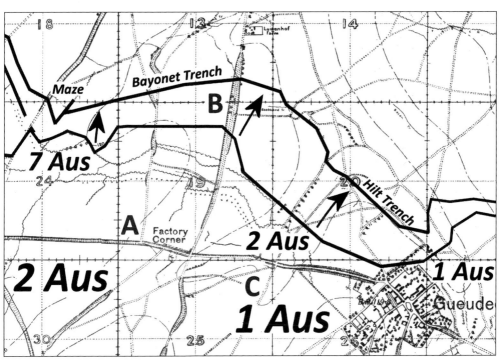

5 November, I ANZAC Corps: While 2nd Australian Division could not capture the Maze, 1st Australian Division was unable to clear Hilt Trench.

13 to 15 November, V Corps

Zero hour was at 5.45am and the troops advanced through thick fog.

3rd Division, Serre
Viewpoint A: Sheffield Memorial Park
Viewpoint B: Serre Road Number 2 Cemetery

Hardly any 2nd Suffolks and 10th Welsh Fusiliers found Serre Trench. Only a few 8th King's Own and 1st Gordons reached Walter Trench. Serre Trench was overrun and everyone fell back across no man's land. The 1st Scots Fusiliers and 2nd Royal Scots lost direction and were pinned down astride the Serre road. The few who made it to the support line soon withdrew.

> 3rd Division, Major General Cyril Deverell
> 8 Brigade, 2nd Royal Scots, 8th East Yorkshires, 1st Scots Fusiliers, 7th Shropshires
> 9 Brigade, 1st Northumberland Fusiliers, 4th Royal Fusiliers, 13th King's, 12th West Yorkshires
> 76 Brigade, 8th King's Own, 2nd Suffolks, 10th Welsh Fusiliers, 1st Gordons
> Pioneers, 20th KRRC: Artillery, XXIII, XL and XLI Brigades

2nd Division, Frankfurt Trench
Viewpoint C: Redan Ridge Cemetery 1

The 2nd South Staffords came under effective fire whilst cutting the wire protecting the Quadrilateral. They then captured the wrong trenches and the 17th Middlesex followed them. The 13th Essex struggled to advance past the Quadrilateral but a few reached Beaumont Trench and blocked Lager Alley.

The 24th Royal Fusiliers and 2nd HLI reached Beaumont Trench but the 2nd Ox and Bucks and 17th Royal Fusiliers veered left and captured Lager Trench, at right angles to their objective. Isolated groups reached Frankfurt Trench but they soon withdrew to Munich Trench and then Beaumont Trench. A few men held on in Crater Lane and Wagon Road. The 22nd Royal Fusiliers established a line facing the Quadrilateral while the 23rd Royal Fusiliers sent reinforcements to Beaumont Trench.

At 6.20am on 14 November the 1st Berkshires and 1st KRRC were hit by their own barrage in the mist. The Berkshires overran Munich Trench

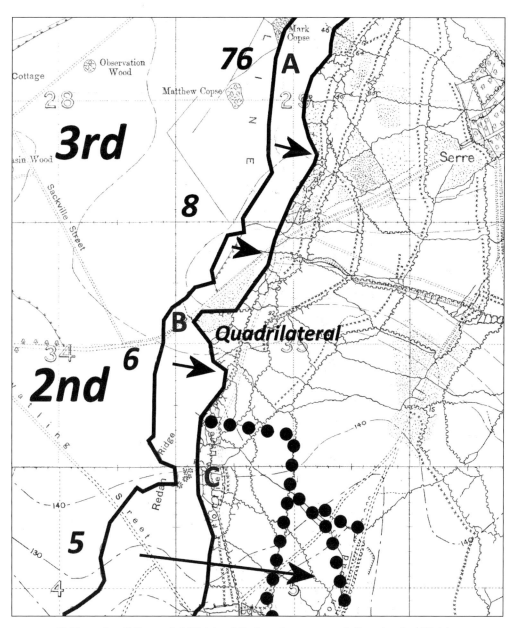

13 November, V Corps: 3rd Division failed to advance towards Serre but 2nd Division made progress on Redan Ridge.

and a few reached Lager Alley and Serre Trench but the KRRC drifted right into Leave Avenue. They both withdrew to Wagon Road while the 22nd Royal Fusiliers covered the flank between the Quadrilateral and Lager Alley. The 11th Warwicks and 6th Bedfords attacked Frankfurt Trench at 2.45pm but were stopped by machine gun fire from Munich Trench and withdrew to Wagon Road. At 9am on 15 November two tanks ditched while the 8th East Lancashires and 10th Loyals lost their way trying to find Munich Trench in sleet.

2nd Division, Major General Charles Monro

5 Brigade, 17th Royal Fusiliers, 24th Royal Fusiliers, 2nd Ox and Bucks, 2nd HLI

6 Brigade, 1st King's, 2nd South Staffords, 13th Essex, 17th Middlesex

99 Brigade, 22nd Royal Fusiliers, 23rd Royal Fusiliers, 1st Berkshires, 1st KRRC

Pioneers, 10th DCLI: Artillery, XXXIV, XXXI and XLII Brigade Attached from 37th Division

112 Brigade, 11th Warwicks, 6th Bedfords, 8th East Lancashires, 10th Loyals

The Caribou in Newfoundland Memorial Park.

13 November, VIII Corps

51st (Highland) Division, Beaumont Hamel and Y Ravine
Viewpoint A: The Argylls memorial on the Sunken Road
Viewpoint B: Newfoundland Memorial Park

The Scots crept through the mist and the barrage started when the mine detonated under Hawthorn Crater at 5.45am. The 1/8th Argylls and the 1/5th Seaforths fought past the crater but their two tanks ditched. The 1/6th and 1/5th Seaforths cleared the north part of Beaumont Hamel while the 1/6th Gordons mopped up behind.

The 1/6th Black Watch were pinned down at the west end of Y Ravine but some entered Beaumont Hamel. The 1/7th and 1/5th Gordons started clearing Y Ravine while some of the 1/5th Gordons reached Station Road. The 1/4th Gordons surrounded the gully as men of the 1/6th and 1/7th Black Watch cleared it. They all then moved through Beaumont Hamel as the 1/5th Gordons formed a defensive flank. The 1/7th Argylls and 1/9th Royal Scots entered Munich Trench but artillery fire forced them out.

> 51st (Highland) Division, Major General George Harper
> 152 Brigade, 1/5th and 1/6th Seaforths, 1/8th Argylls and 1/6th Gordons
> 153 Brigade, 1/6th and 1/7th Black Watch, 1/5th and 1/7th Gordons
> 154 Brigade, 1/4th Seaforths, 1/4th Gordons, 1/9th Royal Scots, 1/7th Argylls
> Pioneers, 1/8th Royal Scots: Artillery, CCLV, CCLVI and CCLX Brigades

Memorial B: The 51st Division memorial is at the north end of the Newfoundland Memorial Park.

63rd (Royal Naval) Division, West Bank of the Ancre
Viewpoint C: Station Road, between Beaumont Hamel and the Ancre

The 1st and 2nd Royal Marines and the Howe and Anson Battalions were pinned down in no man's land and only a few reached Station Road. The Hawke and Nelson Battalions took heavy casualties but the Hood and Drake Battalions captured the front trenches. Lieutenant Colonel Bernard Freyberg of the Hood Battalion led everyone he could find to Station Road and

Beaucourt station next to the river. The 1st Honourable Artillery Company (HAC) captured the Mound and then advanced along the river bank. Few 10th Dublin Fusiliers, 4th Bedfords and 7th Royal Fusiliers reached Beaucourt Trench because the rest were busy fighting the Germans in the front line trenches.

63rd (Royal Naval) Division, Major General Cameron Shute
188 Brigade, Anson Battalion, Howe Battalion, 1st Marines, 2nd Marines
189 Brigade, Drake Battalion, Hood Battalion, Nelson Battalion, Hawke Battalion
190 Brigade, 1/1st HAC, 7th Royal Fusiliers, 4th Bedfords, 10th Dublin Fusiliers
Pioneers, 14th Worcesters: Artillery, CCCXV, CCCXVII and CCCXVIII Brigades

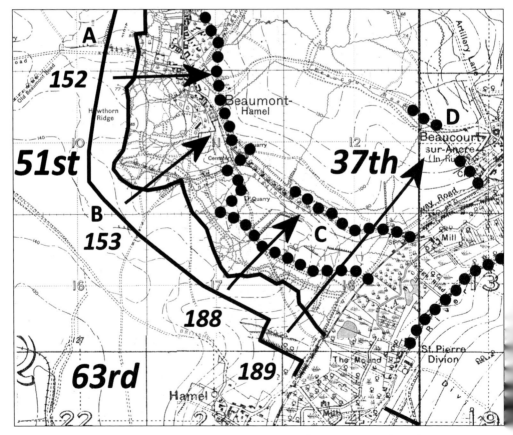

13 November, VIII Corps: While 51st Division cleared Beaumont Hamel, 63rd Division advanced along the west bank of the Ancre towards Beaucourt.

13 November, II Corps

Zero hour was before dawn and mist was expected, so innovative sound signals were arranged to synchronise the infantry advance with the artillery barrage. The gun batteries would fall silent to give the troops a five-minute warning; it also gave the gunners a short rest. When the artillery started firing as fast as possible, it was time to advance again.

39th Division, the Hansa Line
Viewpoint A: Station Road east of Beaumont Hamel; view across the Ancre
Viewpoint B: Pope's Nose emplacement, west of Helen's Tower

One tank broke down and two ditched, leaving the 16th Sherwoods to advance into St Pierre Divion, at 6.15am. The 17th Sherwoods secured the hamlet and Mill Lane Trench beyond. The 4/5th Black Watch veered down the slope while the 1/6th Cheshires lost the benefit of the barrage in the mist and took time to clear the Strasburg Line. The 1/1st Cambridge's left reached Mill Trench and established an outpost at Beaucourt mill. The Cambridge right and the 1/1st Hertfords cleared the Hansa Line. The 7th Loyals helped to dig a new trench in front of the Hansa Line while the 14th Hampshires looked after over 1,300 prisoners. The strongpoint at the junction of Mill Road and the Hansa Line was finally captured at 6.45pm.

> 39th Division, Major General Gerald Cuthbert
> 116 Brigade, 11th, 12th and 13th Sussex, 14th Hampshire
> 117 Brigade, 16th and 17th Sherwoods, 17th KRRC, 16th Rifle Brigade
> 118 Brigade, 1/6th Cheshires, 1/1st Cambridge, 1/1st Hertfords and 4/5th Black Watch
> Pioneers, 13th Gloucesters: Artillery, CLXXIV, CLXXIX, CLXXXIV, CLXXVI Brigade

19th (Western) Division, the Hansa Line
Viewpoint C: Beaucourt civilian cemetery
Viewpoint D: North of Thiepval cemetery

The 7th Loyals reached the Hansa Line, where they were reinforced by the 7th King's Own. Field guns hit the Germans along the sunken road called

Lucky Way and the 7th East Lancashires mopped up. The 6th Wiltshires could not reach Stump Road, so they dug in east of Lucky Way.

> 19th (Western) Division, Major General Tom Bridges
> 56 Brigade, 7th King's Own, 7th East Lancashires, 7th South Lancashires, 7th Loyals
> 57 Brigade, 10th Warwicks, 8th Gloucesters, 10th Worcesters, 8th North Staffords
> 58 Brigade, 9th Cheshires, 9th Welsh Fusiliers, 9th Welsh, 6th Wiltshires
> Pioneers, 5th South Wales Borderers: Artillery, LXXXVI, LXXXVII and LXXXVIII Brigades

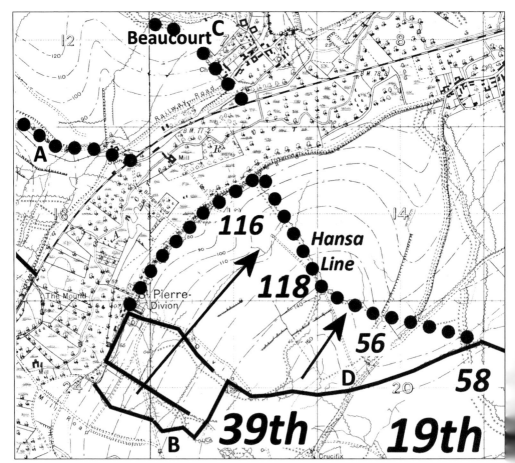

13 November, II Corps: 39th and 19th Divisions advanced to the Hansa Line on the east bank of the River Ancre.

14 to 15 November, VIII Corps

51st (Highland) Division, Munich Trench
Viewpoint A: New Munich Trench British Cemetery

Orders to attack at 6.20am on 14 November arrived too late for the 1/7th Argylls to take part and the 1/9th Royal Scots failed to clear Leave Avenue. The two battalions entered Munich Trench at 7.30am but a combination of British and German artillery fire forced them out. The Scots dug a trench overnight called New Munich Trench only to find the Germans had abandoned Munich Trench the following morning. The few 1/7th Argylls who reached Frankfurt Trench, in appalling conditions, had to withdraw.

> 51st (Highland) Division, Major General George Harper
> 152 Brigade, 1/5th and 1/6th Seaforths, 1/8th Argylls and 1/6th
>   Gordons
> 153 Brigade, 1/6th and 1/7th Black Watch, 1/5th and 1/7th Gordons
> 154 Brigade, 1/4th Seaforths, 1/4th Gordons, 1/9th Royal Scots,
>   1/7th Argylls
> Pioneers, 1/8th Royal Scots: Artillery, CCLV, CCLVI and CCLX
>   Brigades

Memorial B: 51st (Highland) Division's flagpole memorial is in the centre of Beaumont-Hamel.

63rd (Royal Naval) Division, West Bank of the Ancre
Viewpoint C: Beaucourt civilian cemetery

At 6.20am on 14 November the 13th Rifle Brigade and the 13th Royal Fusiliers advanced from Station Road through the mist towards Beaucourt Trench. The Rifle Brigade then bombed towards Leave Avenue. Men from the 13th KRRC, HAC and 7th Royal Fusiliers spent the day clearing Beaucourt, with the help of the 14th Worcesters. They captured over 500 prisoners and Lieutenant Colonel Bernard Freyberg was awarded the Victoria Cross for leading the attack. Three tanks had been sent forward but one was disabled and two ditched; one crew stayed with their tanks and continued to fire their guns until 400 prisoners surrendered to the 10th Dublin Fusiliers. The Howe Battalion also discovered 200 Germans sheltering in dugouts along Station Road.

63rd (Royal Naval) Division, Major General Cameron Shute

188 Brigade, Anson Battalion, Howe Battalion, 1st Marines, 2nd Marines

189 Brigade, Drake Battalion, Hood Battalion, Nelson Battalion, Hawke Battalion

190 Brigade, 1/1st HAC, 7th Royal Fusiliers, 4th Bedfords, 10th Dublin Fusiliers

Pioneers, 14th Worcesters: Artillery, CCCXV, CCCXVII and CCCXVIII Brigades

Memorial D: The 63rd (Royal Naval) Division memorial is at the western end of Beaucourt.

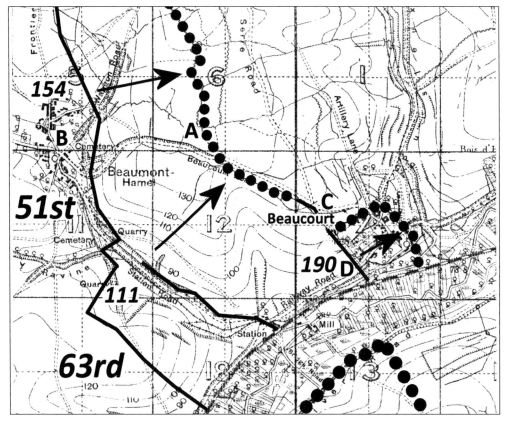

14 to 15 November, VIII Corps: 51st Division advanced east of Beaumont Hamel as the 63rd Division cleared Beaucourt.

16 to 18 November, VIII Corps

32nd Division, Munich Trench
Viewpoint A: New Munich Trench British Cemetery

On 16 November 32nd Division took over Redan Ridge and linked up with 51st Division in New Munich Trench. At 6.10am on 18 November the 15th HLI failed to bomb along Ten Tree Alley but the 2nd Manchesters entered Lager Alley in sleet. One company followed Serre Trench to the village where they were surrounded and fought to the last man. The 2nd KOYLIs' left company advanced past the junction of Lager Alley and Munich Trench but the right company could not reach Munich Trench. The 16th HLI's left reached Frankfurt Trench but the right of the battalion and the 17th HLI were pinned down. Few Highlanders made it back from their isolated position.

> 32nd Division, Major General William Rycroft
> 14 Brigade, 19th Lancashire Fusiliers, 1st Dorsets, 2nd
>   Manchesters, 15th HLI
> 96 Brigade, 16th North'd Fusiliers, 15th and 16th Lancashire
>   Fusiliers, 2nd Inniskillings
> 97 Brigade, 11th Borders, 2nd KOYLIs, 16th and 17th HLI
> Pioneers, 17th Northumberland Fusiliers: CLV, CLXI and
>   CLXVIII Brigades

37th Division, Muck Trench
Viewpoint B: Beaucourt civilian cemetery
Viewpoint C: 750 metres east of Beaucourt, turn left up the slope to Bois d'Hollande

On the morning of 15 November, 13th Rifle Brigade bombed along Beaucourt Trench, linking up with 51st Division in Munich Trench. The Germans abandoned Muck and Railway Trenches north-west of Beaucourt but Muck Trench was deep in mud. On 16 November the 10th Royal Fusiliers bombed to the junction of Frankfurt Trench and Leave Avenue while the 13th KRRC advanced along Railway Trench. The 8th Somersets and 4th Middlesex cleared Puisieux Trench, meeting men of 19th Division on the Ancre. That night the 8th Somersets advanced along Ancre Trench towards Bois d'Hollande, north-east of Beaucourt.

On 18 November, the 10th Royal Fusiliers bombed to the junction of Frankfurt Trench and Leave Avenue while the 13th KRRC advanced along Railway Trench. The 8th Somersets and 4th Middlesex also cleared Puisieux Trench.

37th Division, Major General Bruce Dickenson
63 Brigade, 8th Lincolns, 8th Somersets, 4th Middlesex, 10th
    York and Lancs
111 Brigade, 10th and 13th Royal Fusiliers, 13th KRRC, 13th
    Rifle Brigade
112 Brigade, 11th Warwicks, 6th Bedfords, 8th East Lancashires,
    10th Loyals
Pioneers, 9th North Staffords: Artillery, CXXIII, CXXIV and
    CXXVI Brigades

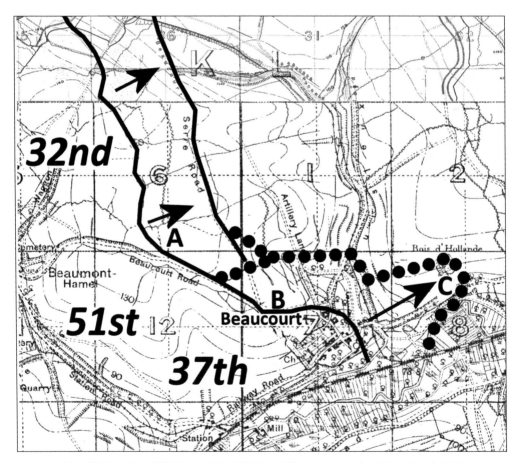

16 to 18 November, VIII Corps: 32nd Division failed to capture Frankfurt Trench, 37th Division advanced beyond Beaucourt.

14 to 18 November, II Corps

19th (Western) Division, Battery Valley
Viewpoint A: Battery Valley, on the road from Thiepval to Grandcourt

On 14 November wire stopped the 7th South Lancashires reaching Lucky Way but the 9th Welsh entered Stump Road. German attempts to recapture Schwaben Redoubt on 16 November failed.

On 18 November the 7th South Lancashires advanced along the Grandcourt road and contacted the troops in Beaucourt across the river. The 7th East Lancashires also met troops along the railway line but they could not reach Baillescourt Farm, north of Grandcourt. The 8th Gloucesters crossed Battery Valley and the Grandcourt Line and entered Grandcourt, meeting the South Lancashires. The 10th Warwicks' left entered Grandcourt but the right was stopped by wire. The 8th North Staffords also crossed the Grandcourt Line but most were surrounded in the village. The 9th Cheshires failed to capture Desire Trench.

The 7th South Lancashires stopped a counter-attack at the west end of Grandcourt on 19 November. All the troops later withdrew to a less exposed trench across Battery Valley; but the Grandcourt Line still overlooked them. The 10th Royal Fusiliers were able to capture the vantage point during the afternoon.

19th (Western) Division, Major General Tom Bridges
56 Brigade, 7th King's Own, 7th East Lancashires, 7th South
    Lancashires, 7th Loyals
57 Brigade, 10th Warwicks, 8th Gloucesters, 10th Worcesters, 8th
    North Staffords
58 Brigade, 9th Cheshires, 9th Welsh Fusiliers, 9th Welsh, 6th
    Wiltshires
Pioneers, 5th South Wales Borderers: Artillery, LXXXVI,
    LXXXVII and LXXXVIII Brigades

18th (Eastern) Division, Desire Trench
Viewpoint B: Stump Road Cemetery near Grandcourt

One 7th Queen's detachment was destroyed along the Stump Road but the rest of the battalion reached Desire Trench in a blizzard. The Buffs were pinned down in no man's land until the 7th Queen's Own captured their objective and the 8th East Surreys reached Desire Trench. The 7th Queen's and the 7th Buffs had to withdraw to Regina Trench and a trench was dug from it to Desire Trench.

18th (Eastern) Division, Major General Ivor Maxse
53 Brigade, 8th Norfolks, 8th Suffolks, 10th Essex, 6th Berkshires
54 Brigade, 11th Royal Fusiliers, 7th Bedfords, 8th Northants,
    12th Middlesex
55 Brigade, 7th Queen's, 7th Buffs, 8th East Surreys, 7th Queen's
    Own
Pioneers, 8th Sussex: Artillery, LXXXII, LXXXIII, LXXXIV and
    LXXXV Brigades

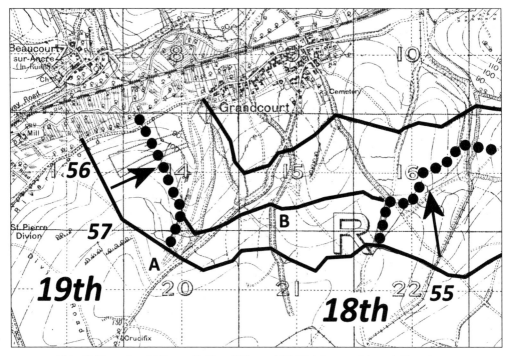

14 to 18 November, II Corps: Neither 19th nor 18th Divisions could reach Grandcourt.

10 to 18 November, Canadian Corps

4th Canadian Division, Regina Trench
Viewpoint A: Gravel crossroads beyond Regina Trench Cemetery
Viewpoint B: Adanac Cemetery

The Canadians crept forward under a clear moonlit sky on 10 November. At midnight the 46th, 47th and 102nd Canadian Battalions overran the east part of Regina Trench.

On 18 November the 38th, 87th, and 54th Canadian Battalions advanced from Regina Trench, across Desire Trench and to Desire Support. But 75th Canadian Battalion became disorientated in the sleet and crossed the Pys road. The 44th and 47th Canadian Battalions reinforced the front while patrols entered Grandcourt Trench; they refused to leave until the following morning. The 50th Canadian Battalion reached Desire Support but 46th Canadian Battalion was pinned down. It meant 50th Battalion had to withdraw from its isolated position.

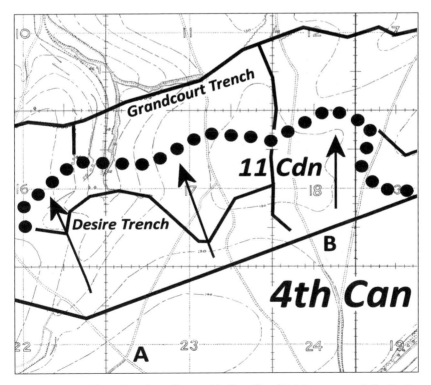

10 to 18 November, Canadian Corps: 4th Canadian Division captured the Desire Trenches and could have also taken Grandcourt Trench but were ordered to withdraw from it.

4th Canadian Division, Major General David Watson
10 Brigade, 44th, 46th, 47th and 50th Canadian Battalions
11 Brigade, 54th, 75th, 87th and 102nd Canadian Battalions
12 Brigade, 38th, 72nd, 73rd and 78th Canadian Battalions
Pioneers, 67th Canadian (Pioneer) Battalion: Artillery, V, XI and
    XVIII Brigades

The Canadian Corps

All four divisions of the corps were engaged around Thiepval and Courcelette between the end of August and mid-November. Their endeavours are remembered by the Canadian Memorial at Courcelette. They suffered over 24,700 casualties and the names of the missing are carved on the panels of Vimy Ridge's memorial to Canada's missing, near Arras.

Thiepval Memorial to the Missing.

Index